Transnationalism in the Balkans

After a decade of exclusive nationalism, violence and isolation of the 1990s, the Balkans has seen the emergence of transnational links between former ethnic foes. Do these new cross-border links herald the era of inter-ethnic reconciliation in place of the politics of ethnic exclusion? Are they proof of a successful transition from authoritarianism and war to democracy and peace? Drawing on substantial empirical research by regional specialists, *Transnationalism in the Balkans* provides a sobering insight into the nature of cross-border links in the region and their implications. Several of the authors show how transnational connections in the context of weak states and new borders in the region have been used by transnational networks – be it in politics, economics and culture – to undermine a democratic consolidation, perpetuate state weakness and keep the practice of exclusive ethnic politics and identities alive. These findings make a strong case to go beyond the region and put forth a critical argument for rethinking the theories of transition to democracy in the post-Communist and post-conflict setting to incorporate a dimension of globalisation.

This book was previously published as a special issue of *Ethnopolitics*.

Denisa Kostovicova is a lecturer at the Department of Government and Development Studies Institute, and a fellow at the Centre for the Study of Global Governance at the London School of Economics and Political Science. She received a Ph.D. from Cambridge University in 2002. Her research interests include nationalism and democratisation in the global age, post-conflict reconstruction and security, and the European integration of western Balkans. She is the author of *Kosovo: The Politics of Identity and Space* (Routledge, 2005).

Vesna Bojicic-Dzelilovic is a research fellow at the Centre for the Study of Global Governance at London School of Economics and Political Science. Her main area of research and teaching is the political economy of war and post-war reconstruction. She has a Ph.D. in Economics.

T0295999

Transnationalism in the Balkans

Edited by
Denisa Kostovicova and Vesna Bojicic-Dzelilovic

Routledge
Taylor & Francis Group

LONDON AND NEW YORK

First published 2008 by Routledge

2 Park Square, Milton Park, Abingdon, Oxon OX14 4RN
711 Third Avenue, New York, NY 10017, USA

Routledge is an imprint of the Taylor & Francis Group, an informa business

First issued in paperback 2016

Typeset in Times Roman by Techset Composition, Salisbury, UK

British Library Cataloguing in Publication Data
A catalogue record for this book is available from the British Library

ISBN13: 978-0-415-46446-8 (hbk)
ISBN13: 978-1-138-98607-7 (pbk)

Contents

Transnationalism in the Balkans: An Introduction

Transnationalism and the Balkans have been two very exciting fields of study in recent years. Despite vast scholarship in both areas, they still appear to produce distinct results. With the support of Volkswagen Stiftung, the Centre for the Study of Global Governance, the London School of Economics and Political Science (LSE), and the Institute for East European Studies, Free University, Berlin organized the conference 'Transnationalism in the Balkans: The Emergence, Nature and Impact of Cross-national Linkages on an Enlarged and Enlarging Europe' at the LSE in November 2004. The aim of the conference was to analyse, from a multi-disciplinary and international perspective, the ongoing process of transnationalization of the Balkans on the path of its integration in Europe. Transnationalism ties heterogeneous Europe into a functioning and workable political and geographic whole through the creation of cross-border linkages that foster cooperation despite persisting national differences. Applying the concept of transnationalism has allowed us to take a conceptually fresh look at the transformation of the Balkans and to complement the scholarship on the region. At the same time, while regular interactions across national boundaries comprise the essence of transnational relations, transnationalism has been conceptualized broadly to encompass trans-societal and trans-governmental relations (Risse-Kappen, 1995). The collected articles in this issue not only shed insight on the changing political, economic and cultural dynamics in the Balkans, they also place and investigate transnationalism in the global age. Alongside speeding up and intensification of transnational relations, its chief characteristic is the nation-state's loss of dominance as a political actor. Its consequence is the pluralization of spaces for the flourishing of transnational relations including a myriad of non-state actors.

This transformation of nation-state is of particular relevance in the post-communist context. Democratization of East Central European countries itself implies a reform of an omnipresent communist state, the expansion of the civil society, and the pluralization of identity politics. The profound change is embedded in increasingly intense transnationalization in the global context, which as the articles demonstrate offers both a positive and negative impetus for the post-communist democratization.

The traditional territoriality and sovereignty of nation-states, shaping the notion of national identity, are all being presently unbundled. A clear distinction between domestic and foreign affairs is now fuzzy, while political communities are not defined primarily in territorial terms. Anderson likens the end of state sovereignty and territoriality in the globalizing world to the new medievalism. He particularly refers to different levels of overlapping sovereignty constituting nested hierarchies where the territories of medieval European states were discontinuous without fixed borders (Anderson, 1996). This process shapes the form of transnational relations which no longer involve just states.

Mandaville (1999) borrows Appadurai's notion of *translocality* to underscore that it is not the rejection of territory and place as a space of politics that has taken place in a global age, but a change in the nature of understanding the boundaries of the territory. He points out the disjuncture between 'one's legal identity as a citizen of a territorial state and one's political identity as an actor in the public sphere' (ibid., p. 657). Ultimately, the territory and state no longer create limits to politics and identity (ibid., p. 654). By contrast, the politics becomes transnational, sustained by increasing transnational linkages and identities.

Importantly, the change of state territoriality and sovereignty has not as yet heralded the demise of the state, but rather its transformation. In the context of globalization, as Anderson (1996, p. 135; cf. Pringle, 1998) points out, 'we need to think of the state and its sovereignty in the plural rather than the singular'. Studying the EU, scholars have reflected on the de-statization of political regimes by elaborating a shift from 'government to governance on various territorial scales and across different policy fields' (Heeg and Ossenbrugge, 2002). Governance is no longer a vertical top–down process emanating from the parliament but becomes a matter of coordination between a multitude of actors on horizontal levels in form of partnerships, networks and alliance. Notably, the partnerships include governmental, para-statal and private organizations (ibid., p. 82).

Multi-level governance has also led to the relativization of scales—without a privileged geographical scale—whether on local, regional, national or supranational level. As a consequence, scholars have noted a necessity of 'jumping scales' as new forms of social solidarity and alternatives to neoliberalism. Thus, transnational linkages cross borders but also pair up with partners at a variety of levels creating a web of interlinkages, producing, as this issue demonstrates, a variety of outcomes.

Beck (2000) has noted that the unity of the national state and national society comes unstuck in the globalized world characterized by the transformation of the traditional notion of the nation-state. Such a disconnect creates a space for flourishing civil society that is now connecting and expanding transnationally (Kaldor, 2003). On the one hand, civil society provides yet another field for the forging of transnational connections, both among its activists and through arrangements of cooperation with states and governments. On the other hand, the growth of the global civil society contributes to the pluralization of the spaces of politics, and identities they forge.

European integration is a process quintessentially based and built on the cross-border interaction. When viewed from the perspective of identity, 'Europeanization', i.e. the multi-level political integration of nation-states within the EU, is not straightforward. Scholars have demonstrated that, Europeanization may introduce a greater political consciousness of Europe, but can also be paralleled by the process of nationalization, as the policy-makers are forced to formulate national positions and vital interests (Johansson, 1999). This issue disects a contradictory impact of transnationalism in relation to the Balkans' quest for integration into the European Union, that is used as a stimulus both for forces advancing and obstructing a democratic change. Only a handful of scholars have looked at the process of transnationalization in the context of East Central Europe (Desoldato, 2002; Thaler, 2001; Baldersheim *et al.*, 2002), and even fewer have applied a transnationalism lens to the Balkans. Addressing transnationalism in the context of the post-communist Eastern Europe, Verdery has argued that a 'transnational travel' of some concepts such as citizenship and private property may undergo a local transformation, and actually lead to their nationalization. Effectively, rather than reinforcing democratization, it may be perverted in the local context to actually challenge it (Verdery, 1998).

Transnationalism as a conceptual tool allows insight into the type of interconnectedness arising in the post-communist transition states. The Balkans' integration into Europe is taking place against the backdrop of the rapidly changing external context that, at the same time, becomes internal. Europeanization along with initiatives focused on regional cooperation, have significantly displaced the isolationism of the period of nationalist mobilization and war of the 1990s. However, the region's aspiration to join the European Union is also having a polarizing effect between and within the states. European integration creates winners and losers in the regional context, but also figures prominently as a hotly contested issue within states. This particularly concerns the conditionality related to cooperation with the International Criminal Tribunal for the former Yugoslavia. Hence, the establishment of transnational linkages in the Balkans as part of the post-communist and post-conflict transformation must be viewed in a wider context of the recent wars in former Yugoslavia as its distinct feature. The 'European' ideal has manifested itself as a desire for the European future of nation-states in the Balkans, but is premised on a strong sense of national identity.

As an analytical concept, transnationalism provides insight into the impact of two-way contact and interaction between the linkages, rather than viewing Europeanization as a one-way transfer of values from the West towards the East. Importantly, this does not deny the existence of common values, rights and principles that underpin the European integration process. In the Balkan context, a transnational perspective that includes an acceptance of and engagement with the national Other can provide insight into the processes of confronting and overcoming ethnic tensions and animosity resulting from the conflicts in the 1990s.

The Balkans, and, especially, the Yugoslav successor states and Turkey, are of particular interest, because both their compatibility with the West and their ability to adapt to 'Western' values have been questioned in the context of European integration. The peoples of the Balkans define themselves as European. Joining Europe has figured prominently on the political agenda of their elites. However, their actual commitment to the 'European dream' has been strikingly uneven in the region, despite the official rhetoric to the contrary. The process of European integration has to be accompanied by a multiplication of cross-border and transnational links across the region in order to be meaningful, effective and feasible.

As the articles in this special issue demonstrate, emerging transnational relations in the Balkans are diverse, encompassing a variety of both state and non-state actors. At the same time, their impact on the European integration is ambiguous. The creation of transnational civil society networks has to a certain extent contributed to inter-ethnic reconciliation and tolerance in a war-torn region, furthering the process of European integration. By contrast, the flourishing of transnational criminal links in the Balkans during and after the bloodshed has undermined the democratization of new states and entities in the region, obstructed inter-ethnic reconciliation and stymied the advance towards the European Union.

In their contribution, Kostovicova and Bojicic-Dzelilovic argue that the 'troubled' Europeanization of the region, characterized by the post-communist and post-conflict transition, can be explained by viewing globalization as internal to transformation through the impact of transnational networks on perpetuating state weakness in the Balkans. Informal networks that link political, military and security establishment with criminal groups, transcend ethnic and national boundaries, and represent the most challenging legacy of the war and its political economy, influencing transition in the Balkans. These networks depend on inter-ethnic cooperation, yet, at the same time, stirring ethnic tensions is vital for their survival. The impact of this dynamic is ambivalent: on one hand, formal regional cooperation is stifled and, in some spheres, e.g., the economy, the emphasis is on developing formal links with Europe rather than within the region. On the other hand, the informal transnational links, including those with an illegal/criminal slant, are dense, integrating the region into global illicit flows. This latter aspect is elaborated in the paper by Hozic, who addresses this unintended transnationalization from its long historical perspective.

External incentives have been a driving force behind the emergent transnational links engaging civil society, which somewhat modify the paucity of transnational linkages in the region. While acknowledging the positive developments in this segment, Devic, in her paper, provides an insight into why external initiatives have failed to engage already existing forms of civil society in Kosovo. According to her, the promotion of multi-ethnic coexistence and transnational relations by non-governmental organizations in Kosovo has been difficult because both Albanian and Serbian elites have prioritized a political zero-sum game of sovereignty and ethnocentric citizenship. Baker provides a perspective on transnational relations between the former Yugoslavian successor states from the point of view of popular music, and demonstrates how transnational musical figures are interpreted as symbolic reference points in national ethno-political discourse.

Finally, two papers by Winland and Bulut focus on transnationalism in the context of diasporic politics. The role of diaspora in the Balkans has been ambiguous at best. Winland looks at the role of transnational diasporic communities in response to the aspiration of the homeland to join the EU, and argues that Croatia's Europeanization was premised on the marginalization of the Croatian diaspora in Canada in stark contrast to its mobilization and input during Croatia's quest for independence. Lastly, analysing sizeable communities of Balkan descent in Turkey and their role in forging cross-border links between Turkey and the Balkans since 1989, Bulut shows how such individuals and groups have increasingly become subjects in relations between Turkey and the rest of the Balkans. However, alongside this process, precisely as trans-state ties have increased in significance, Bulut argues, the 'state' has attempted to harness or infiltrate the 'trans-state' to further state interests.

Ultimately, the collected articles make a strong case for challenging the concept of transnationalism, both on the grounds of its meaning and of its impact in the context of globalization. They raise two key questions: what does 'transnational' mean when the actors involved in cross-border interactions no longer privilege a nation-state, but rather draw it into a complex relationship with non-state counterparts?, and how can transnationalism as a positive force fostering democracy be reconciled with transnationalism as a negative force obstructing it? This issue provides no easy or simple answers to either. While Kostovicova and Bojicic-Dzelilovic show that a transnational pull by the European Union is a crucial anchor for democratic consolidation of the Balkans, Hozic shows that the region's global integration will inevitably entail its incorporation into the illicit flows. Devic tackles the argument that the transnational impetus to civil society development implies a promotion of democracy and shows that it may actually further entrench the ethnification of politics. Lastly, exploring the Balkan diasporas, Winland underscores a contradictory implication of different 'kinds' of transnationlism. While the Europeanization encourages dense cross-border linkages, these are mainly directed at the European Union and at the expense of those with the Croatian diaspora, which had their hey day during Croatia's struggle for independence. Lastly, Bulut draws attention to the state's response to increasing transnationalization occurring at the grass-roots levels and its attempt to reclaim transnationalism to pursue its own interests.

References

Anderson, J. (1996) The shifting stage of politics: new medieval and postmodern territorialities?, *Environment and Planning D: Society and Space*, 14(2), pp. 133–153.

Baldersheim, H., Bucek, J. & Swianiewicz, P. (2002) Mayors learning across borders: the international networks of municipalities in East-Central Europe, *Regional and Federal Studies*, 12(2), pp. 126–137.

Beck, U. (2000), *What is Globalisation?* (Cambridge: Polity Press).

Delsoldato, G. (2002) Eastward enlargement by the European Union and transnational parties, *International Political Science Review*, 23(3), pp. 269–289.

Heeg, S. & Ossenbrugge, J. (2002) State formation and territoriality in the European Union, *Geopolitics*, 7(3), pp. 75–88.

Johansson, K.M. (1999) Europeanisation and its limits: the case of Sweden, *JIRD*, 2(2), pp. 169–186.

Kaldor, M. (2003) *Global Civil Society* (Cambridge: Polity Press).

Mandaville, P.G. (1999) Territory and translocality: discrepant idioms of political identity, *Millenium: Journal of International Studies*, 28 (3), pp. 653–673.

Pringle, D.G. (1998) Globalisation, reterritorialisation and national identity, *Geopolitics and International Boundaries*, 3(3), pp. 1–13.

Risse-Kappen, T. (1995) Bringing transnational relations back in: Introduction, in T. Risse-Kappen (Ed.) *Bringing Transnational Relations Back In: Non-state Actors, Domestic Structures, and International Institutions*, pp. 3–33 (New York: Cambridge University Press).

Thaler, P. (2001) Fluid identities in Central European borderlands, *European History Quarterly*, 31(4), pp. 519–548.

Verdery, K. (1998) Transnationalism, nationalism, citizenship, and property: Eastern Europe since 1989', *American Ethnologist*, 25(2), pp. 291–306.

Europeanizing the Balkans: Rethinking the Post-communist and Post-conflict Transition

DENISA KOSTOVICOVA & VESNA BOJICIC-DZELILOVIC

The 2004 Eastern enlargement of the European Union (EU), in which eight post-communist states became members of the EU, changed the map of Europe profoundly. However, the European future of their counterparts in the Balkans is still uncertain, despite the unprecedented push the EU instigated to set the Balkan partners on the European path in 2005. It has given the go-ahead to accession negotiations with Croatia and kicked off negotiations on a Stabilization and Association Agreement with Serbia and Montenegro; meanwhile, Bosnia-Herzegovina has advanced internal reforms to be able to follow suit. Does this development lay to rest recent warnings that the Balkans, or, to be precise, Bosnia-Herzegovina, Serbia and Montenegro, Kosovo and the Former Yugoslav Republic of Macedonia,[1] may become "an EU enclave" or a "ghetto" (Lehne, 2004, p. 123; 'Breaking out of the Balkan ghetto', 2005)? For a long time, the prospect of EU membership has failed to energize a large swathe of the Balkans to commit to an effective and focused reform programme, confounding expectations among policy makers and analysts. The latest engagement in the region has introduced a contractual basis for relations between the EU and the states and entities of the region. However, their profound political, economic and social transformation, dubbed Europeanization, has yet to take place. Crucially, this process will not be determined purely by domestic forces, but by transnational ones, too. The effectiveness of the EU's approach in the region will be determined to the extent that it successfully counters the interplay between internal and transnational dynamics at play. Only then will the fears of a 'Balkan ghetto' be dispersed.

We argue that globalization provides a missing link in an explanation of the troubled post-communist and post-conflict transition in the Balkans. Focusing on the impact of transnational networks as global actors that thrive in the permissive environment of weak states in the Balkans, the paper demonstrates that globalization is internal to the post-communist and post-conflict transition in the region. In sum, globalization is not just a context that moulds the unfolding transitions, but also a force that shapes them from within. Ultimately the paper argues that the Europeanization of the Balkans, which can be taken as a measure of success of the unfolding political and economic reforms, has been stalled because the transnational dimension of transition in the region has been underestimated in the European Union's approach to the Balkans.

In this paper we approach the transition literature as a dominant paradigm informing the EU's approach to the Balkans, and examine it with particular interest in terms of its application to the Balkan case. While agreeing with the scholars who identify 'stateness' and the international dimension as areas calling for further elaboration in the post-communist democratization literature applied to the Balkans, we show that this literature is chiefly characterized by an elaboration and expansion of analysed dimensions rather than by a radical rethink of their manifestation and impact on transition. The paper then examines the Balkan transnational space and the role of transnational actors in the process of transition. Lastly, it shows that, in a global age, transnational networks can thwart political and economic reform processes and, accordingly, the transformation of a weak post-communist and post-conflict state into a strong state, which, in turn, perpetuates the issue of state cohesion.

Europeanization of the Balkans: Approaches to Post-communist Transition

With its legacy of communism and conflict, the European integration of the western Balkans has posed a unique policy challenge to the EU. Transition and stabilization have been set as two explicit aims for the region's European integration process. Consequently the EU has developed a strategic enlargement as well as a security concept for the Balkans, along with the corresponding instruments (Lehne, 2004). The cornerstone of this policy has been the Stabilization and Association process (SAp). As a policy instrument, the SAp has been tailored since 1999 to match the double challenge of post-communist and post-conflict transition in the Balkans. It has built on the accession approach applied to Central and Eastern Europe with a policy of enhanced conditionality and regional cooperation. Both these instruments have proved wanting.

What we call 'enhanced conditionality', spanning political, economic and '*acquis*'-related requirements of membership, as well as conditions emanating from peace agreements and political deals (Anastasakis & Bechev, 2003; Smith, 2003, pp. 113–114), has favoured states that have made the greatest progress in reform. This, in turn, has created a new line of division in the region between Balkan candidates and 'potential candidates'. No policy follow-up was designed to fill the vacuum created by the success of the individual aspirants (Papadimitriou, 2001). Nor, as van Meurs points out, could tensions and asymmetries thus caused be compensated by regionality (van Meurs, 2000, p. 22; cf. Demetropoulou, 2002).

Indeed, from the start of the process, the European integration of the Western Balkans has been characterized by the 'stability dilemma', i.e. of those countries that suffer from the greatest stability deficits not qualifying for the EU's initiatives (Wittkowski 2000, p. 85). Calic went even further in a critique of the SAp (2003, p. 121). According to Calic, accession-oriented instruments are ill-suited to tackling the region's key problems of state building, conflict resolution and economic growth. In fact, the EU has tackled state building and conflict resolution in the western Balkans, but did so primarily through the evolving tools of the European Security and Defence Policy (ESDP), such as its police and military missions in Bosnia-Herzegovina and Macedonia. Scholars have seen the EU's twin approach to the western Balkans, embodied by the SAp and the ESDP mechanisms, as a demonstration of the EU's growing strength in projecting stability into the region (Vachudova, 2003, p. 157; Yusufi 2004). By contrast, we argue that it has introduced another level of separation of the EU's policy instruments, often interfering with the SAp—as Serbia and Montenegro's example illustrates powerfully. That country's European integration process has been hindered by tensions resulting from the application of the agreement on state union brokered by the EU as a part of the ESDP.

The vacuum created by the EU's approach to the Balkans has crucially benefited a particular group of transnational actors, which has posed a threat to security *and* has spoiled transition efforts, thus undermining the Europeanization of the Balkan states. The effectiveness of criminal networks thriving on the weakness of the Balkan states springs from the fact that they are "multi-ethnic, cross-border and integrated in Europe" (Anastasijevic, 2004). The EU approach, for all its nuances, has not been able to match the sources of strength of the spoilers of Europeanization. Arguably their biggest strength is the exploitation of the weakness of the state and the new borders in the region, including, importantly, those between successful EU candidates and aspirants. The EU's state-building agenda, to the extent that it can be formulated in the variety of instruments that have been used, is ill equipped to address this complex reality on the ground. The EU's regional approach has been piecemeal at best and, essentially, sub-contracted to the Stability Pact, while key initiatives with regional implications, such as local war crimes trials, remain confined within state borders. In addition, the EU's engagement in the western Balkans through the ESDP has had an ambiguous effect on advancing European integration precisely because it was not integral to the SAp.

The EU's policy approach has been framed by a conceptual approach to transition, in which, as we show, the role of transnational actors in the post-communist and post-war transition has not received adequate attention. The field of transitology has been informed by the study of transitions from authoritarianism. With its legacy of total state control over politics, economy and society dating from the communist period, the democratization of Eastern Europe and the former Soviet Union raised a question: can the existing scholarship on transition be applied to its post-communist variant?[2] This debate had not yet been resolved when a new challenge was thrown up: a striking divergence in the transitional experience of Central and Eastern Europe, on the one hand, and of the Balkans and the former Soviet Union, on the other, cried out for an explanation. Post-communism as a common denominator of all these states itself failed to provide an answer.

The following paragraphs provide a brief overview of approaches to post-communist transition to democracy in general, and to transition in the Balkans in particular. We argue that the troubled transition in the Balkans can be explained by analysing it in conjunction with globalization. Without an agreed definition of globalization (cf. Held & McGrew, 2000), for the purpose of our argument, two aspects of globalization—conceived of as a complex process unfolding in politics, economics and culture—are particularly relevant: interconnectedness and transnationalism.[3] Interconnectedness is closely related to the erosion of the boundary between the domestic and the external aspect of politics in the global age, while intensification of transnational relations creates not only transnational spaces of politics but also transnational networks that permeate the domestic political arena (Beck, 2000; Kaldor, 2003; Giddens, 2002). Globalization, which has not been theorized in the transition literature, arguably has a decisive impact on transition in post-communist countries because transnational actors, and the relations they create, encroach on the domestic sphere and become *innate* to transition. Furthermore, a transnational perspective allows us to explain why a 'stateness' issue persists in the Balkan case. Linz and Stepan note that there is a 'stateness' problem "when there are profound differences about the territorial boundaries of the political community's state and profound differences as to who has the right to citizenship in that state" (1996, p. 16). Specifically we posit that state weakness needs to be theorized as a key issue in the transition in the Balkans and as an explanation for a persistent question of state legitimacy deriving from a nationalist challenge to the territorial framework of the state.

Very soon after the demise of communism, Offe (1991) summarized the complexity of the post-communist transformation succinctly, dubbing it a 'triple transition' that encompasses democratic and economic liberalization coinciding with a quest for the creation of new nation-states. Subsequently the literature has built around the approach focused on the mode of transition, the design of democratic institutions and the political elites and participation, and the approach emphasizing the impact of the communist legacy on shaping the political, economic and social transition in Eastern Europe and the former Soviet Union.[4] These approaches are distinguished by the thrust of their respective arguments rather than by a complete exclusion of competing explanations. Common to both has been an awareness of the interconnectedness of multidimensional processes of post-communist democratic consolidation, including the challenge posed by their simultaneity (Pridham, 2001). Nonetheless, three key themes have emerged from this literature: simultaneous democratization and marketization; 'stateness'; and the international dimension.

Post-communist democratization literature on the Balkans built on the East and Central European literature in two directions. A comprehensive analysis of democratization in the Balkans, in an edited volume by Pridham and Gallagher, highlighted the impact of the historical legacy alongside the simultaneity of three types of transformation: political, economic and that linked to nation building (Pridham & Gallagher 2000). This dimension encompasses both the pre-communist and communist legacy. As the authors demonstrate, it affects the transition through various forms: political culture, civil society (and a lack of it), political leadership, prior democratic experience, etc. To capture diverse transitional paths in the Balkans, Pridham advocates an interactive approach with a "dynamic potential that is particularly attractive as it allows us to bring into play such determinants as the historical and how legacies from the past impact on the present as well as the interplay between top-down dictates and bottom-up pressure" (2000, p. 6; Cf. Vučetić, 2004).

The other line along which post-communist democratization literature has been adapted to account for the Balkan 'anomaly' problematizes the 'stateness' dimension (cf. Szabo, 1994; Sekelj, 2001). Kopecký and Mudde (2000) called for a better understanding of the distinct processes of state- and nation building and of the international dimension, encompassing both the context and the actors, and their role in post-communist democratization. Echoing Offe's approach, Kuzio (2001) proposed a 'quadruple transition', advocating a separate analysis of 'stateness', interpreted as state-institution building, and 'nationness', deemed civic nation building. Indeed, the stability of a state's political and territorial framework, whether theorized in terms of Linz and Stepan's 'stateness' or in terms of state-destroying ethnic nationalism (Parrott, 1997), is one of the key distinguishing features of post-communist democratization. Nevertheless, the unanswered question in the Balkan case is: why do the issues of 'stateness', national cohesion and state weakness persist? Are they related and how? Does multi-ethnicity *a priori* thwart the prospects of democratic consolidation (cf. Roeder, 1999)?

The focus on the pre-communist and communist legacy singles out a set of dimensions that prominently figure in Balkan democratization. Even though it was bumpy, Romania's and Bulgaria's road towards European integration provides a sobering view of the constraining impact of these legacies. However, it also brings to the fore the impact of war in the Balkans as a post-communist legacy on post-communist democratization. Arguably the wars in the 1990s shaped both the pre-communist and communist legacy in politics, economics and society in the Balkans. Enumerating war-related difficulties of transition in the western Balkans, Batt singled out the destruction of social capital; distorted economic liberalization; state weakness caused by the growth of military and security forces and corruption; social transformation as a result of forced migration; and a lack of trust in the political elites (2004, pp. 18–19). Mungiu Pippidi (2005) highlights a destructive impact that informal networks in status-based societies can have on social trust as the essence of social capital (see also In Search of Responsive Government, 2003). While the legacy of war provides an important analytical avenue, we argue that its explanatory power is undermined by excluding a global dimension of the legacy of the war and its impact on democratic transition and, consequently, on the European integration of the Balkans.

The international aspect of democratization has been criticized as an underestimated and under-theorized aspect of transition to democracy (cf. Wiarda, 2000). The literature here subsequently took up the transnational aspect of post-communist democratization. Schmitter's observation on the actors in the promotion of democracy has been particularly relevant for the post-communist experience. Referring to international organizations, human rights groups, foundations, the media, transnational firms, dissidents, etc., he pointed out that "this world beneath and beyond the nation-state has played an especially significant role in the international promotion of democracy" (Schmitter, 1996, p. 29). It is this complexity of 'external' actors on the democratic consolidation that the contributions in Zielonka and Pravda's (2001) edited volume sought to illuminate (cf. Brown, 2000; Lewis, 1997; Cichock, 2002). The literature on the international and transnational dimension of post-communist transition and democratization has sought to explain the moulding of domestic processes under the impact of external actors and contexts. Crucially this literature maintains the distinction between the domestic and the external, albeit somewhat mitigated by the impact of the external on the domestic (Cf. Pravda, 2001, p. 6; Pridham *et al.*, 1994). We contribute to the analytical effort by changing the perspective on the internal and external elements of politics. We relate the post-communist democratization in the Balkans to globalization, a process that erases the distinction between the internal and the external.

We demonstrate in this paper that 'stateness'—conceptualized both in terms of nation- and institution building and in a dialectical relationship between the two—continues to plague democratization efforts in the Balkans because of the impact of transnational networks. They are both internal and external in the context of globalization. These networks are a product of 'new wars', which, as Kaldor (2001) argues, are inextricably linked to globalization, and owe their resilience in the post-war phase to a combination of a weak state and integration into global transnational networks. Their relation with a multi-ethnic nature of their local environment is ambivalent. While they depend on collaboration with members of other ethnicities, they are apt to stir ethnic tensions lest stabilization should favour the imposition of the rule of law and their sanctioning. In sum, inter-ethnic collaboration is necessary to sustain their activity, but stirring ethnic tensions creates an environment in which they project themselves as a guarantor of their own ethnic group's security. Ultimately the issue of 'stateness' presents itself as the impossibility for ethnic groups to achieve a consensus on the state and nation, when its root cause should actually be sought in the mode of operation of transnational networks.

Ethnic Networks and Weak State: The Transnational Context and Transition in the Balkans

The weak state in the Balkans is a key to understanding the operation of the transnational networks through a deleterious linkage between political and economic interests. We therefore argue that it is not so much the simultaneity of democratization and marketization, but rather their conflation and exploitation by the political elites in the Balkans, that are obstacles to the transitional efforts. Without the rule of law all economic acts are political. This dimension cannot be understood without an elaboration of economic informality in the Balkans. Here we draw on Krastev's (2002) conceptualization of a weak state in the Balkans. According to him, the Balkan state is weak in four different ways. The first relates to Migdal's (1988) theory, conceiving of state weakness as the inability of governments to implement their policy visions, to penetrate society, to regulate, etc. The second relates to citizens' view of a state. Specifically, a state may be able to collect taxes and be strong in that respect, but be unable to deliver the rule of law or protect human and property rights. The third approach defines a weak state as being captured by particular political interests that dominate policy. And the fourth stems from the strategic behaviour of elites involved in a predatory project that extracts resources from the state. By implication, in post-communist Balkan states, while there have been elections and a change of elites, there has also been a preparedness to strip the state bare. The state weakness in the Balkans has had a decisive impact on democratization in the region. However, there have been no attempts to integrate this within the transitional framework of Balkan transition, despite its recognition as a problem (Cf. Muço, 2001; Sotiropoulos, 2001).

While critiquing the analysis of state weakness in isolation from globalization in the transition literature, we benefit from the literature on post-communist democratization, which underlines the importance of the pre-communist and communist legacy. Importantly we relate it to the war legacy as well. Examining the impact of transnational actors in the context of a weak state, we explain the perpetuation of particularist nationalist politics, while placing the transition paradigm in a broader environment of globalization. We now turn to the Balkan transnational space and look at how it has been reconfigured more recently as a result of local–global dynamics and, in that context, at the implications of the rise to prominence of a particular group of transnational actors on the region's transition trajectory.

The Legacy of a Common State

The break-up of the common economic and political space through the dissolution of former Yugoslavia, once the largest country in the Balkans, has added a specific twist to the transnational context against which the newly created countries set out to implement transition reforms. Having transformed themselves from federal units of a single state into independent political entities, former Yugoslavia's successor states have found it difficult to extricate their economic, social and political being from the experience of belonging to a common state. The geopolitical reconfiguration of the Balkan space has fundamentally transformed the nature and patterns of interaction of state- and non-state actors alike. The very notion of what is external and/or international in the national governance framework has become somewhat ambivalent in this context, bearing a specific weight in the structuring of Balkan transnational relations.

Despite the high degree of decentralization of former Yugoslavia's particular model of socialism, decades of development under the unifying ideology of the communist state and its centrally planned economy had created a basic set of country-wide economic and political institutions, and a web of dense and diverse links among its various communities, peoples and institutions. The existence of the common state allowed for unhindered flows of people, capital and information as the foundations of the single economic space, in which a country-wide specialization was nurtured through the system of central planning. This political system gave former Yugoslavia's constituent people an equal status, extending the same political, cultural and economic rights irrespective of where the administrative borders of former Yugoslavia's republics cut across these communities. The creation of the five independent states on the territory of former Yugoslavia, and the imposition of state borders, brought this model to an end. Production chains were cut and enterprises split by these new borders; commercial links were severed and the very nature of commercial transactions were altered through the disappearance of a common currency; new minorities were created, becoming the new states' diaspora communities. In this changed context the legacy of a common state, by way of once intense and diverse links, familiarity with institutions, common culture, language similarities and spatial proximity, proved a facilitating factor for all sorts of transactions, often motivated by more-or-less similar concerns shared by the population. But by far the most buoyant were transactions based around exploiting the differences between newly bordered political entities and their relations as independent states with third parties (e.g. the European Union). The greater the attempt to control these borders, the greater the incentive to create informal transactions. The tightening of the EU's immigration policy had the same effect.[5] In the economic domain these transactions have as a rule tended to evolve along informal and/or illicit trade routes, since formal cross-border activities have been constrained by the combined effects of the economic impact of transition, subsequent wars and hostile politics between the new neighbours. With regard to the former, output contraction, similarity of production structures and European trade incentives resulted in modest economic cooperation across the new borders; indeed, in their changed economic outlook, the newly established countries appeared more like competitors. Ethnic politics imposed additional constraints on the more vigorous development of formal economic exchange and acted as a potent restraining factor in cross-border interaction in other fields.

The legacy of a common state has been reflected in the actual implementation of the transition policies. For example, with the disappearance of a common state, the issue of explicitly domestic governance, such as privatization, becomes internationalized. Assets which are the subject of privatization as well as the key actors of privatization are now separated by the borders of several states and state- like entities, which makes the implementation of this key transition policy reform more intricate than in other countries and undermines its standing as domestic policy in its own right. Similarly the implementation of human rights provisions as part of a democracy-building agenda has acquired international clout because of the way in which the various policy concerns have been affected by the creation of new borders. The very disappearance of a common state triggered substantial migration flows, which escalated further with the onset of the wars of the 1990s. For their host states dealing with the claims of these new migrants has required complex inter-state procedures in response to the specific concerns of their status and rights created by the disintegration of former Yugoslavia.

These two examples highlight the unique significance that the legacies of belonging to a common state have in shaping the Balkan countries' transformation trajectories in their transnational context. They point to the importance of understanding developments in the Balkans' political, economic and social spheres in their idiosyncratic regional context, where a common history, culture and physical proximity mean continued diverse and complex links across newly created borders, escaping the logic of nation-bound policies informing approaches to Balkan transition. The legacies of belonging to a common state not only affect the linkages among various actors both at the state and sub-state level within former Yugoslavia's space, but also affect a definition of the terms and dynamics of the Balkan countries' broader transnational relations, including, most concretely, EU and NATO membership, cooperation with the International Criminal Tribunal for the former Yugoslavia and various other international agencies.

The Legacy of War and its Political Economy

The involvement of a large array of external actors in the 'wars of Yugoslav succession'— a common term denoting a series of conflicts on the territory of former Yugoslavia—can be traced at every stage of these conflicts. It ranged from the engagement by the major

powers, neighbouring states, international governmental and non-governmental organisations and international business to diasporas and organized crime and terrorist networks.
The modalities and intensity of this engagement differed among the individual actors; their
mutual relations, too, mutated and transformed with the ebbs and flows of the conflict. But,
in the process, they played a defining role in repositioning the Balkans in the global setting
through the particular way in which they were integrated ('domesticated') into the logic
and mode of operation of local politico-economic and social structures.

The political dynamics created through the war had a distinctly transnational dimension; sustaining the war momentum required participation of actors at different territorial
levels linked in the complex patterns of interaction. Looking from a purely internal and
resource-focused perspective, given the restricted financial and combat resources of the
warring parties, some of whom, moreover, were constrained by an international arms
embargo, the outbreak of the conflict and its conduct was possible only because of its
outward opening. Thus arms, and other combat and everyday goods, foreign fighters
and money came from across the borders, providing vital input for waging the war. Humanitarian aid poured in to help the victims of violence, and an international civilian and
military presence intensified as the conflicts subsided. Goods came into the conflict
zone only partially using formal channels, often travelling along peace-time smuggling
routes and pathways that had been adapted to the war-fighting needs. Flows of money followed a similar pattern. Often money was carried in the personal luggage of individuals
acting in various official and non-official capacities, or found its way to its recipients
through real and fictitious entities.[6] Another factor contributing to the thickening web
of cross-border interactions that developed under the cover of the war were international
sanctions against Serbia and Montenegro for its involvement in the wars in Bosnia-
Herzegovina and Croatia. Sanction busting, which provided a lifeline to the regime in Belgrade, brought together a whole gamut of transnational actors who engaged in the very
lucrative, yet clandestine, trade in all sorts of legal goods, especially those carrying a
high tariff premium, e.g. fuel, cigarettes and alcohol, aided and sponsored by that regime.

The growth of informal transaction in the Balkans, which will become the most
complex issue of its post-conflict transformation, was not just a side effect of war, as
seems to be largely the case in classic inter-state wars. In fact, the character of the violence
itself, which had its roots in the disintegration of the state structures, defined the economic
mode on which it was sustained. The failure of the state to provide for the public opened
the space to alternative supply networks. The weak taxation basis of the formal local
economy prompted a search for alternative sources of economic power secured through
informal economic practices. For the most part initially this involved the clandestine
trade of mainly legal goods but, increasingly, illegal ones were also involved. It also
included the appropriation ('taxation') of humanitarian assistance, as well as various
other more or less sophisticated schemes outside conventional production and exchange.
An important source of funding was secured through diaspora networks, some of which
were directly linked to criminal rings (e.g. Albanian diasporas' funding of the Kosovo
Liberation Army). Recourse to informality was a common occurrence during communist
times, which made the foundation for the new system that much easier. What changed was
the nature of informality, in that the outright criminal enterprise became its substantial part
and transformed into a phenomenon whereby it was no longer possible to delimit formal
from informal economic space.[7] The importance of this mutation is partly to do with the
size, i.e. the expanding zone, of the criminal economy. The other, equally sinister, aspect is

the way in which state structures became engaged in criminal activities, either by direct involvement or through their complicit behaviour,[8] and the long-term damaging impact this has had on building the legitimate institutions of governance on which the EU approach to stabilization of the region rests.

The informal enterprise, which formed the core of the Balkan war economy, was fuelled and sustained through multiple links integrating into global chains of informal trans-border trade, of which criminal trade is a part.[9] It provided a source of living for large numbers of ordinary people struggling to survive war-inflicted destitution, and a source of profit for those within politico-military structures or with privileged access to them. The main figures of this emerging non-regulated economic space, who grew to wield important political influence, were people close to the politico-military establishment, regardless of whether they were individuals with a criminal past, members of diasporas, or conventional tradespeople. Often they were bound together by the bonds of ethnicity, kinship or political affiliation. Goods looted locally, which frequently belonged to opposing ethnic group, were shipped to foreign markets through networks of agents operating transnationally (like the footloose agents, this type of transaction is, by its very nature, non-territorial). They crossed paths with goods stolen world-wide, with narcotics, with people and other commodities circulating within global clandestine trade rings in which the Balkans' role grew as the prospect of stability remained distant.[10] Part of the proceeds from the sales were plugged back into fighting the war. The Balkans' war economy provided an economic power base for the state and state-like entities engaged in violence. It was through various forms of clandestine activity,[11] in which ethnic elites colluded and actively interacted across borders and linked into global informal trade flows, that the new political regimes could be sustained. The close links between political, military, security and criminal elites, linked into networks operating across borders, represent the most challenging legacy of the war and its political economy. They are influencing the process of transition in the Balkans and are something to which the EU approach has so far failed to provide an adequate response.[12]

The Impact of Liberal Economic Reforms

Economic liberalization, as a potent channel through which the forces of globalization work, is another important force shaping the transnational context of the Balkan transition through pressures on the countries to implement liberal economic reforms as part of the post-communist transition. At their core, the externally assisted transition programmes have an economic reform package based around neoliberal economic precepts of deregu-lation, liberalization and privatization as the key to the establishment of a market-based economy. Indeed, the creation of the market economy based on a neoliberal restructuring agenda is the essence of the SAp itself (and of the EU accession process in general) and a point of reference for defining conditionality criteria. The reforms are aimed at eliminating the interference of the state in the economic domain and transforming its role into that of a regulator of the market-based economic regime. Liberal economic reforms also presup-pose a particular model of development in which exports and foreign investment are viewed as crucial to improving competitiveness. Exposed to this particular paradigm, Balkan countries are pressed to privatize state-owned assets, deregulate their markets and remove barriers to trade. To the degree that the reforms are implemented, they are supposed to provide the Balkans with the benefits of access to capital, technology and markets, and presumably provide an opportunity for a different pattern of integration into a world economy than the one characteristic of the pre-transition phase. This essentially means that the territorial outreach within which economic development takes place has broadened, and that the role of the factors on which it depends has been redefined, accentuating the importance of the non-national, non-state arena for their utilization. Where actors are concerned, this transformation opens the possibility for a profound encroachment of international commercial and financial capital into the Balkans' domestic economic sphere—a tendency underpinning the overall logic of neoliberal globalization. The manner in which the process of reforms is guided—through the involvement of a complex set of inter-linked institution such as the international financial institutions and the EU—makes it impossible to consider it solely a matter of domestic policy.

The economic and political setting against which economic reforms have been pursued in the Balkans is a complex one, in which the legacy of underdevelopment and over-sized industry is compounded by war-induced disruption and political instability. It is the region that has historically lagged behind the developed part of Europe that constitutes the core of the European Union.[13] The Balkans' insertion into the world economy in the pre-transition period was based on a narrow export capacity, mainly in semi-processing and extractive industries, which were particularly hard hit in the process of transition. The sheer scale of restructuring required to turn the economy towards one in which exports will provide the key engine of growth is monumental for poor countries—including most of the Balkans. In trying to (re)capture external markets, they have faced strong competition, finding it difficult to achieve and maintain a competitive edge. The fiscal and monetary austerity required by the reforms has constrained the state's capacity to provide public services, resulting in the reduction of breadth of public services and a decline in quality. Another particularly important aspect of the Balkan transition has been the scale and persistence of unemployment in the aftermath of the years of conflict in the region, and restricted job opportunities. This has made it even more problematic for neoliberal reforms to deliver the professed benefits of these reforms. Rather, a sharp increase in poverty and inequality has been one of the distinct features of transition in this region, which, in the post-conflict environment, is becoming even more disconcerting in both its economic and its political repercussions. The extent of penetration of foreign capital in the Balkans has been limited; in terms of the scale of foreign investment, the Balkans have attracted a significantly smaller inflow of foreign investment than the Central European transition economies. Rather than through greenfield investment in productive capacity, foreign capital has come mainly through privatization, especially in the banking sector. The concentration of foreign ownership in the more lucrative segments of the economy increases the political influence of transnational capital, while defining the pattern of economic transformation and therefore the position of the Balkans in the world economy. Thus far the limited inflow of new strategic investment has constrained corporate restructuring and most Balkan countries have failed significantly to improve their competitive position as a mark of any strengthened economic stance.

To carry out the complex agenda that neoliberal economic restructuring entails requires a state capacity—in terms of institutions, resources and political commitment—that, as the analysis in the first part of this paper highlighted, most Balkan states lack. Economic liberalization, against the background of a war economy and weak state, had the unintended effect of perpetuating and nurturing the type of transnational links that have not contributed to stabilizing the region through greater cooperation.

Transnational Actors

The above three instances, each representing a channel through which globalization has had a distinct influence on Balkan contemporary development, combine to create a context within which powerful groups of transnational actors who shaped the course of transition have nestled. The multiplication of borders, migrations, including forced population displacement, the war economy and the perverse impact of neoliberal adjustment have provided a fertile ground on which these actors were able to expand their activities.[14] It is a context marked by economic under-development, ethno-criminal politics and inadequate local capacity to forge ahead with the process of modernization that the EU agenda has implicitly come to signify.

While none of the actors is new or unique to the Balkans, it is important to point out that reshaping their identities, motives and, consequently, the nature of the impact of their agency can only be grasped with reference to this context. For example, diasporas, by definition a transnational actor (Ostergaard-Nielsen, 2001, p. 218) in this context become actively involved in local politics not only through traditional channels of influence such as political lobbying, donations and remittances (all of which were amply used in the Balkans), but also by participating directly in matters of internal governance. The case in point is the parliamentary representation of diasporas in Croatia. This in turn fundamentally redefines the parameters within which diasporas operate, making them a potent force that can influence political outcomes in the domestic arena from within the borders of a home state.[15] The practice of members of diasporas taking on government office has been widespread in the region, compared with isolated cases in other transition countries. During the conflicts, diasporas provided funding, manpower, connections to international political and military circles, and logistics support for waging the war. Diaspora funding has been an important source for sustaining local economies and shoring up government budgets. This latter aspect was particularly important during the conflicts, with implications for their dynamics as well as for the political re-grouping against which the conflict settlement had to be devised. For example, in the case of quasi-state authorities such as the Bosnian Croat para-state of Herzeg-Bosnia, diaspora funding played a pivotal role in establishing parallel structures of government that proved the key obstacle in implementing the peace agreement.[16] Similar problems were encountered in Kosovo and, in less institutionalized form, within Bosnian Serb and Bosnian Muslim structures, as well as in Serbia and Macedonia. While undoubtedly easing the life of ordinary people, the impact of these funds, often channelled through political party structures, can be quite different in terms of a government's credibility in fulfilling its role. This type of support attenuates the constraints a weak economy imposes on the fiscal basis of the state, and modifies the basis of the contract between the government and the public. Being an alternative source of funding, it can make the government less susceptible to external pressure to pursue reform aimed at improving fiscal position.[17] Of course, not all modes of diaspora engagement can be viewed solely in terms of feeding into conflict dynamics; there are examples of positive and constructive diaspora engagement in the Balkans. The point is, rather, that the many varied ways in which the diaspora has been engaged in the Balkans provides an important part of the explanation for the tenacity of ethno-national structures, as diasporas generally follow lines of ethnic affiliation.

The plurality of actors, and the diversity and variety of trans-border activities, make it difficult to consider any of them in isolation. So, for example, diasporas are often closely associated with organized crime;[18] transnational non-governmental organizations are sometimes linked to international financial agencies; terrorist organizations often secure some of their funding through organized crime and are sometimes linked with seemingly benevolent non-governmental organizations, and so on. Instead, it is more appropriate to conceive of transnational actors operating as a complex system of overlapping networks, which work in concert with (and through) local structures. Giving this system functional integrity is the mode by which these networks have been accommodated within local structures, providing the vital resource for the sustenance of a particular type of political authority that has emerged in the Balkans under the impact of post-totalitarian transition, conflict and globalization.

Going back to the key question of the causes of state weakness in the Balkans addressed earlier, in this way one can get a better insight into the role organized crime and terrorist networks, as a particularly ominous and dangerous transnational phenomenon, have come to play in the local social dynamics. Such a focus can also provide a more accurate understanding of how, through these networks, the initiatives aimed at strengthening formal structures of governance are captured and subverted, making these structures empty shells that ultimately cannot perform the tasks required by the EU accession agenda.[19]

Duffield (2001) talks about form of authority that do not require, or indeed imply, territorial control, and Jung (2003) refer to it as a concurrence of shadow state and shadow economy. The essence in which this form of political authority differs from a conventional notion of (functioning) state is that real power resides in the informal structures that are built around (and through) the formal institutions of the state, and that do not have their economic power base in regular economic activity. This type of political authority can only be sustained in the transnational and global context. The growing literature on new wars views the emergence of this type of political authority as closely following the dynamics of globalization, even referring to it as 'shadow globalization' (Jung, 2003) because of the importance that informal and criminal structures play in sustaining it. This type of political authority has no interest in strengthening state institutions and forging regional cooperation, both of which are instrumental for the success of the EU strategy towards the Balkans.

Organized crime is, by its nature, transnational in its outlook and has been fuelled by the ease of communications and opportunities that the process of globalization has opened. The nature of the activity makes the zones of instability, in which legal and political order is weak, its natural habitat.[20] In this sense the Balkans have been a strong pole of attraction for organized crime. However, its development into a relevant force decisively influencing economic and political dynamics in the Balkans is intricately related to the establishment of the new forms of political authority following the collapse of Yugoslavia and the region's subsequent difficult transition. It is not just a case of organized criminal groups or, for that matter, diasporas, protruding into the Balkan political, social and economic space. These groups found eager interlocutors in the new political elite in search of alternative sources of political and economic power, and using ethnic violence as an instrument. The extent of participation of state structures and/or their collusion with organized crime, which has its roots in their near symbiosis during the conflicts, is a particularly sinister aspect of the impact of organised crime on transition in the Balkans.[21] This is why the discourse on organized crime in the Balkans, which views it as the extreme form of informal activity, separate from the conventional economy and outside the particular political context, belies the true nature of its impact.

A complex relationship has developed between local political elites and local and regional organized crime networks hooked to global criminal flows. The existence of many porous borders, and borders controlled by different ethnic groups, provided a strong incentive for illicit activities, in which inter-ethnic cooperation was common. Thus an informal mode of regional cooperation developed in the Balkans. The strong presence of local criminal groups closely linked to political structures controlling parts of the territory provided unimpeded access to global criminal networks. The merging of criminal and political structures is perhaps best illustrated in the figure of Željko Ražnjatović Arkan—a convicted criminal and warlord turned politician and member of the Serbian government.

The links forged in war follow into peace, as Nordstrom (2004) has persuasively argued. The active participation of state structures in criminal activities, blurring the line between what is formal and informal, has made rule-breaking a norm in conducting economic and political affairs in the Balkans, thereby undermining the legitimacy of the state. This explains why informal activity continues to flourish. Organized criminal activities in the Balkans, in their most extreme form, have intensified compared with the late 1980s and shifted their focus to more traditional forms, such as drug and human trafficking. Many local underworld figures have become important players in the transnational organized crime rings, their links to the political establishment providing them with a degree of immunity and the possibility of channelling some of their proceeds into legal businesses.[22]

In this context economic transition reforms have sometimes had an unintended effect. Liberalization against the backdrop of the state-controlled economy unleashed a fierce scramble for remaining resources, which were mainly concentrated in the public domain. Thus control of the state, through the tenure of public office, became a target of political struggle. Control was secured through informal networks, often based on ethnicity or other ascriptive principles. In the Balkans, therefore, privatization has often been captured by network interests, securing privileged access to those closely connected to the political elites. In many instances insider privatization has been a preferred method, enabling the political elites to turn their position into economic might. Instances of money, originating in illicit activities, being laundered through privatization are common. Similarly, trade liberalization has provided another avenue utilized by the informal power structures to benefit disproportionately by breaking the rules in favour of groups associated with local authorities. Thus, the two key economic reforms aimed at establishing a market economy have been misused by power structures linked to organized crime for their own personal enrichment and as a way of propping up their own power base— often defined along ethnic lines. This largely explains why these structures have no interest in strengthening the rule of law and other formal state institutions. These structures, which developed in the course of the region's adaptation to the challenges and opportunities posed by globalization, present the most formidable obstacle to a consolidation of reforms and to the transformation of these societies into stable democracies and prosperous economies.

Conclusion

Progress in the Europeanization of the Western Balkans has been disproportionately slow and uncertain, especially when gauged against the efforts, policies and incentives the

European Union has offered the region since the Kosovo war in 1999. Yet, despite the EU's substantial involvement in and impact on democratization in the region, both the EU's incentives to the western Balkans—through enlargement and ESDP instruments—seem to have actually undercut its ability to project stability in the region. There is some doubt over the EU's commitment to full future membership for the Balkan states. Moreover, its instruments and structures have often been mutually enfeebling rather than reinforcing.

Specifically, our criticism of the EU's approach to the western Balkans concerns the lack of transnational dimension in dealing with the region and, more importantly, in acknowledging the successful advance of some states over others. The creation of insiders and outsiders in the 'EU club' of member states has led to the creation of new borders in the Balkans. These borders delineate areas of a weak rule of law that are swiftly exploited by transnational networks. Rather than strengthening the state to enable it to engage in the Europeanization process, these networks subvert the assistance for inclusion in the EU to advance their own agendas and interests. This explains why formal regional cooperation championed by the EU is only marginal and superficial. Simply put, the EU has not managed to tackle the source of strength of the region's shady transnational networks by countering their transnationalism with a transnationalism of its own. The EU's policy ought to be of the same transnational nature as the activities of the networks that are undermining the European project in the region.

The weak state in the Balkans provides a conceptual nexus for the study of democratic transition in the global age. The separation between the notions of state- and nation building in the literature on democratization of the Balkans is important. However, it does not explain why the issue of 'stateness' persists. We have argued that 'troubled' transitional paths in the Balkans ought to be viewed through the prism of globalization. The informal and criminal networks are affecting the transformation of these states from within. Furthermore, the transnational networks operating as global actors effectively demonstrate the 'internalization' of globalization. It is this dimension of transition that has been neglected in the transition literature. To the extent that the impact of global forces has been acknowledged, it has been consigned to an impact of external forces on domestic processes. We have argued that the transnational networks are a manifestation of globalization becoming internal to transition, shaping it from the inside.

Such a reinterpretation of transition in the Balkans also requires a critical look at the notion of the legacy shaping democratization. By focusing on transnational networks, we highlight the relevance of the domestic legacy inherited from communism, and the transnational legacy acquired mainly through war after communism. The Balkan transitions cannot be understood without understanding the region's double legacy—as well as the interaction between these two legacies. Both these legacies affect state- and nation building. On the one hand, thwarted efforts at state building undermine nation building. On the other, exclusive national interests interfere with the state-building project. They are mutually formative through the activities of networks and the involvement of state structures in these networks. In sum, networks benefit from a weak state and perpetuate the very weakness that sustains them.

The impact of transnational networks prevents the creation of a modern state 'independent of the ruler and the ruled', and manipulates multi-ethnicity into an exclusive politics of fear rather than liberal multiculturalism, ultimately keeping a European future at bay. Key to this is the involvement of the state structures in the informal economy, which itself feeds on illicit transnational flows. Informal and formal are as indistinguishable as economic and political. Thus the state breaks the rules it is supposed to set and enforce. As a result, the state's legitimacy is compromised and the base for building a functioning state eroded. The EU's approach, defined by state boundaries and centred on formal political and economic institutions, while not recognizing their informal side, leaves room for transnational actors to slip through the policy net. As a result, EU engagement in assisting post-communist, post-conflict state building in the Balkans in a global context could have the opposite effect of rekindling the process of fragmentation innate to state building, through ethnic violence.

Notes

1. Macedonia will be used in the continuation of the text as an abbreviated form of 'the Former Yugoslav Republic of Macedonia'.
2. The debate was fired up by the exchange between Valerie Bunce and Terry Lynn Karl and Phillippe C. Schmitter in the *Slavic Review* (Bunce 1995a; Karl & Schmitter 1995; Bunce 1995b; cf. Bova, 1991; Fish, 1999; Pridham, 1994; Nodia, 1996; Munck, 1997).
3. While regular interactions across national boundaries comprise the essence of transnational relations, we conceptualize transnationalism broadly so as to encompass trans-societal and trans-governmental relations (Risse-Kappen, 1995).
4. Compare Linz & Stepan (1996) and Huntington (1991) with Stark & Bruszt (1998); Bunce (1999); Fish (1998); Verdery (1996).
5. The geography of the region, positioned on the crossroads between developed Europe and destitute zones to the far east, and the upheaval caused by the war and sanctions, were important contributing factors to explain the illicit flows of people and goods.
6. Often these were non-governmental organizations with a broader agenda than officially professed, or legally established foreign offices of local states, e.g. some of the embassies of Bosnia-Herzegovina were used for illicit transfers of money destined towards funding the war.
7. Sapir (2000) defines this process as 'economic criminalization'.
8. All types of state structures directly or indirectly became a part of this 'criminal enterprise': security forces, customs officers, bureaucrats, high-ranking politicians and members of government.
9. Balkan transition has been characterized by a sharp and prolonged output decline, so that trade rather than production became the main economic activity. Chavdarova (2001) describes how the shift from work to transactions is conducive to the spread of informal economic practice.
10. Commenting on the importance of understanding the transnational context in which contemporary wars take place, Nordstrom (2004, p. 150) makes the point that there are many actors implicated in the "fortunes of political instability".
11. Andreas (2004) identifies clandestine trade as an arena of ethnic cooperation and conflict.
12. These links were not entirely new; while small-scale and isolated before the conflict, they became ubiquitous in the course of the war. Duffield has argued that the war is "an axis around which social, economic and political relations are measured and reshaped to establish new forms of agency and legitimacy" (2001, p. 136).
13. Recent research shows that, in terms of GDP per head in purchasing power parity (PPP), the position of a number of countries in the region has deteriorated compared with the EU15 in 1910–2004 (cf. Kekic, 2005).
14. This holds true for both types of actors: those with an informal/criminal slant and others such as service-delivery NGOs, which took over the provision of some of the services normally provided by the state.
15. The outcome of Croatian elections has at times been determined by the diaspora vote.
16. Funding from the Croatian state to Bosnian Croat structures extended informally during 2000; from then on much smaller amounts were redirected through the Bosnian Federation government structures. Funding from Croat diasporas continues, with initiatives promoting the goal of Bosnian Croat autonomy.
17. The provision of services by international non-governmental organizations can have a similar effect.
18. This then provides a direct route through which organized crime becomes an actor influencing local processes.

19. The reasons for the poor effectiveness of some internationally sponsored schemes are organizational issues, inadequate funding and, in the case of development assistance, corruption.
20. Organized crime also flourishes in a strongly interventionist state.
21. Not even Albania which, despite bouts of violence, escaped a full scale conflict, has been safe from it.
22. Severing the links with organized crime has been daunting, even when attempted under international pressure. This was illustrated by the assassination of Serbia's Prime Minister Zoran Dindjić, killed because he was attempting to clamp down on organized crime.

References

Anastasakis, O. & Bechev, D. (2003) EU conditionality in south east Europe: bringing commitment to the process, South East European Studies Programme (SEESP), St Antony's College, University of Oxford.

Anastasijevic, D. (2004) Study Group on Europe's Security Capabilities, Brussels, 17 March.

Andreas, P. (Ed.) (2004) Special issue, 'Transnational crime in the Balkans', *Problems of Post-Communism*, May–June.

Batt, J. (2004) Introduction: the stabilisation/integration dilemma, in: J. Batt (Ed.), *The Western Balkans: Moving on*, pp. 7–20, Chaillot Paper, No. 70.

Beck, U. (2000) *What is Globalization?* (Cambridge: Polity Press).

Bova, R. (1991) Political dynamics of the post-communist transition: a comparative perspective, *World Politics*, 44(1), pp. 113–138.

Breaking out of the Balkan ghetto: why IPA should be changed (2005) European Stability Initiative, Berlin, Brussels and Istanbul, 1 June, available at http//:esiweb/org/pdf/esi_document_id_66.pdf.

Brown, A. (2000) Transnational influences in the transition from communism, *Post-Soviet Affairs*, 16(2), pp. 177–200.

Bunce, V. (1999) *Subversive Institutions: The Design and the Destruction of Socialism and State* (Cambridge: Cambridge University Press).

Bunce, V. (1995a) Should transitologists be grounded?, *Slavic Review*, 54(1), pp. 111–127.

Bunce, V. (1995b) Paper curtains and paper tigers, *Slavic Review*, 54(4), pp. 979–987.

Calic, M.-J. (2003) EU Policies towards the Balkans: fostering ownership of reforms, *The International Spectator*, 3, pp. 111–123.

Chavdarova, T. (2001) Corruption in the Bulgarian post-communist transformation, *South-East Europe Review*, 3, pp. 9–18.

Cichock, M. (2002) Transitionalism vs transnationalism: conflicting trends in independent Latvia, *East European Politics and Societies*, 16(2), pp. 446–464.

Demetropoulou, L. (2002) Europe and the Balkans: membership aspiration, EU involvement and Europeanization capacity in south eastern Europe, *Southeast European Politics*, 3(2–3), pp. 87–106.

Duffield, M. (2001), *Global Governance and the New Wars—The Merging of Development and Security* (London: Zed Books).

Fish, M.S. (1998) The determinants of economic reform in the post-communist world, *East European Politics and Societies*, 12(1), pp. 31–78.

Fish, M.S. (1999) Postcommunist subversion: social science and democratization in East Europe and Eurasia, *Slavic Review*, 58(4), pp. 794–823.

Giddens, A. (2002) *Runaway World: How Globalisation is Reshaping Our Lives* (London: Profile Books).

Held, D. & McGrew, A. (2000) The great globalization debate: an introduction, in: D. Held & A. McGrew (Eds), *The Global Transformations Reader: An Introduction to the Globalization Debate*, pp. 1–53 (Cambridge: Polity Press).

Huntington, S.P. (1991) *The Third Wave: Democratization in the Late Twentieth Century* (Norman, OK: University of Oklahoma Press).

In Search of Responsive Government (2003) State building and economic growth in the Balkans, CPS Policy Study Series, Central European University, Budapest.

Jung, D. (2003) *Shadow Globalization, Ethnic Conflicts and New Wars* (London: Routledge).

Kaldor, M. (2003) *Global Civil Society* (Cambridge: Polity).

Kaldor, M. (2001) *New and Old Wars: Organised Violence in a Global Era* (Cambridge: Polity).

Karl, T.L. & Schmitter, P.C. (1995) From an Iron Curtain to a Paper Curtain: grounding transitologists or students of postcommunism?, *Slavic Review*, 54(4), pp. 965–977.

Kekic, L. (2005) The impact of EU membership on East European growth, mimeo. Kekic: EIU (Economist Intelligence Unit) London. Sapir: Ecole des Hautes Etudes en Sciences Sociales, Paris.

Kopecký, P. & Mudde, C. (2000) What has Eastern Europe taught us about the democratisation literature (and vice versa)?, *European Journal of Political Research*, 37, pp. 517–539.

Krastev, I. (2002) The Balkans: democracy without choices, *Journal of Democracy*, 13(3), pp. 49–51.

Kuzio, T. (2001) Transitions in post-communist states: triple or quadruple, *Politics*, 21(3), pp. 168–177.

Lehne, S. (2004) Has the 'Hour of Europe' come at last? The EU's strategy for the Balkans, in: J. Batt (Ed.), *The Western Balkans: Moving on*, pp. 111–124, Chaillot Paper, No. 70.

Lewis, P.G. (1997) Theories of democratization and patterns of regime change in Eastern Europe, *Journal of Communist Studies and Transition Politics*, 13(1), pp. 4–26.

Linz, J.J. & Stepan, A. (1996) *Problems of Democratic Transition and Consolidation: Southern Europe, South America, and Post-Communist Europe* (Baltimore, MD: Johns Hopkins University Press).

Migdal, J. (1988) *Strong Societies and Weak States: State–Society Relations and State Capabilities in the Third World* (Princeton, NJ: Princeton University Press).

Muço, M. (2001) Low state capacity in southeast European transition countries, *Southeast European and Black Sea Studies*, 1(1), pp. 41–54.

Munck, G.L. (1997) Bringing postcommunist societies into democratization studies, *Slavic Review*, 56(3), pp.~542–550.

Mungiu Pippidi, A. (2005) Deconstructing Balkan particularism: the ambiguous social capital in Southeast Europe, *Southeast European and Black Sea Studies*, 5(1), pp. 49–69.

Nodia, G. (1996) How different are postcommunist transitions?, *Journal of Democracy*, 7(4), pp. 15–29.

Nordstrom, C. (2004) *Shadows of War: Violence, Power and International Profiteering in the 21st Century* (Berkeley, CA: University of California Press).

Offe, C. (1991) Capitalism by democratic design? Democratic theory facing the triple transition in East Central Europe, *Social Research*, 58(4), pp. 865–982.

Ostergaard-Nielsen, E. (2001) Diasporas in World Politics, in: D. Josselin & W. Wallace (Eds), *Non-State Actors in World Politics* (Houndmills: Palgrave).

Papadimitriou, D. (2001) The EU's strategy in the post-communist Balkans, *Southeast European and Black Sea Studies*, 1(3), pp. 69–94.

Parrott, B. (1997) Perspectives on post-communist democratization, in: K. Dawisha & B. Parrot (Eds), *The Consolidation of Democracy in East–Central Europe*, pp. 1–39 (Cambridge: Cambridge University Press).

Pravda, A. (2001) Introduction, in: J. Zielonka & A. Pravda (Eds), *Democratic Consolidation in Eastern Europe*, Vol. 2, *International and Transnational Actors*, pp. 1–27 (Oxford: Oxford University Press).

Pridham, G. (2001) Comparative reflections on democratisation in East–Central Europe: a model of post-communist transformation?, in: G. Priham & A. Ágh (Eds), *Prospects for Democratic Consolidation in East–Central Europe*, pp. 1–24 (Manchester: Manchester University Press).

Pridham, G. (2000) Democratization in the Balkan countries: from theory to practice, in: G. Pridham & T. Gallagher (Eds), *Experimenting with Democracy: Regime Change in the Balkans*, pp. 1–23 (London: Routledge).

Pridham, G. (1994) Democratic transition in theory and practice: southern European lessons for Eastern Europe, in: G. Pridham & T. Vanhanen (Eds), *Democratization in Eastern Europe: Domestic and International Perspectives*, pp. 1–37 (London: Routledge).

Pridham, G. & Gallagher, T. (Eds) (2000) *Experimenting with Democracy: Regime Change in the Balkans* (London: Routledge).

Pridham, G., Herring, E. & Sanford, G. (Eds) (1994) *Building Democracy? The International Dimension of Democratisation in Eastern Europe* (London: Leicester University Press).

Risse-Kappen, T. (1995) Bringing transnational relations back in: introduction, in T. Risse-Kappen (Ed.), *Bringing Transnational Relations Back In: Non-state Actors, Domestic Structures, and International Institutions*, pp. 3–33 (New York: Cambridge University Press).

Roeder, P.G. (1999) Peoples and states after 1989: the political costs of incomplete national revolution, *Slavic Review*, 58(5), pp. 854–882.

Sapir J., (2000) Understanding shadow economy and economic criminalization expansion in transition economies: an institutionalist approach, mimeo.

Schmitter, P.C. (1996) The influence of the international context upon the choice of national institutions and policies in neo-democracies, in: L. Whitehead (Ed.), *The International Dimensions of Democratization: Europe and the Americas*, pp. 26–54 (Oxford: Oxford University Press).

Sekelj, L. (2001) National-state and success of democratic transformation in former European communist states, in: D. Berg-Schlosser & R. Vetik, *Perspectives on Democratic Consolidation in Central and Eastern Europe*, pp. 31–45 (Boulder, CO: East European Monographs, distributed by Columbia University Press, New York).

Smith, K.E. (2003) The evolution and application of EU membership conditionality, in: M. Cremona (Ed.), *The Enlargement of the European Union* (Oxford: Oxford University Press).

Sotiropoulos, D.A. (2001) From an omnipresent and strong to a big and weak state: democratization and state reform in southeastern Europe, *Southeast European and Black Sea Studies*, 2(1), pp. 63–74.

Stark, D. & Bruszt, L. (1998) *Postsocialist Pathways: Transforming Politics and Property in East Central Europe* (Cambridge: Cambridge University Press).

Szabo, M. (1994) Nation-state, nationalism, and the prospects for democratization in East Central Europe, *Communist and Post-Communist Studies*, 27(2), pp. 377–399.

Vachudova, M.A. (2003) Strategies for democratization and European integration of the Balkans, in: M. Cremona (Ed.), *The Enlargement of the European Union*, pp. 141–160 (Oxford: Oxford University Press).

van Meurs, W. (2000) The Balkans and new European responsibilities, strategy paper for the Club of Three and the Balkans, 29–30 June, Brussels, available online at: http://www.cap.lmu.de/download/2000/balkan1.PDF.

Verdery, K. (1996) *What was Socialism and What comes Next?* (Princeton, NJ: Princeton University Press).

Vučetić, S. (2004) From southern to southeastern Europe: any lessons for democratisation theory?, *Southeast European Politics*, V(2–3), pp. 115–141.

Wiarda, H.J. (2000) Southern Europe, eastern Europe and comparative politics: 'transitology' and the need for new theory, *East European Politics and Societies*, 15(3), pp. 485–501.

Wittkowski, A. (2000) South-eastern Europe and the European Union—promoting stability through integration?, *South-East Europe Review*, 1, pp. 79–96.

Yusufi, I. (2004) Europeanizing the western Balkans through military and police missions: the cases of Concordia and Proxima in Macedonia, *European Balkan Observer*, 2(1), pp. 8–12.

Zielonka, J. & Pravda, A. (Eds) (2001) *Democratic Consolidation in Eastern Europe*, Vol. 2, *International and Transnational Actors* (Oxford: Oxford University Press).

The Balkan Merchants: Changing Borders and Informal Transnationalization

AIDA A. HOZIC

In the Balkans transnationalism has come to mean either foreign interventions or organized crime. Foreign interventions bring peace and civility to troubled societies. Organized crime, on the other hand, travels through the region like a "fast-spreading virus" whose penetration, through violence and corruption, "diverts resources from the formal economy, undermines the central power essential to make the system work ... and destroys the spirit of social collectivism" (Athanassopoulou, 2004).

However, although usually juxtaposed to each other, the two forms of transnationalism are closely related (Pugh, 2002; 2004). Sanctions and embargoes, just as much as wars, have spurred the growth of underground economies throughout the region (Andreas, 2005). Along with peacekeepers, soldiers and international aid workers, came prostitutes and human traffickers (Mendelson, 2005; Lindstrom 2004; HRW, 2002). With packages of food brought into besieged cities arrived black marketers (Andreas, 2004). Dissolution of old borders and creation of new ones, and particularly the fortification of the (shifting) EU borders, fostered illicit cross-border activities and criminalized some of the previously legal transactions. Working in concert rather than conflict, foreign interventions and organized crime have simultaneously ghettoized the western Balkans while integrating the northern and eastern Balkans into the EU. They have embraced the cosmopolitan urban elites and pushed away the rural poor and, with many of the post-conflict economies still well below EU standards, they have left few options for the majority of the employed and under-employed to join in the world economy except via the vast grey zone of informal trade (Hajdinjak, 2002; Jung, 2003).

Situated somewhere on the continuum between legal, properly taxed economic activity and criminality, the informal economy and tax evasion are the source of major anxieties for the representatives of the international community in the Balkans (GAO, 2000; Bojičić & Kaldor, 1999). In the guesstimates of international organizations, billions of dollars in potential government revenue are allegedly lost every year thanks to the unrestrained growth of the grey economy. Reforms of customs regulations, tax systems and the police are constantly being demanded by the global governance missionaries. And yet, with the spread of informal markets and trading networks, the Balkans has witnessed the rise of a new merchant class—from street vendors and peddlers to major wholesalers; the reconstitution of internal markets, which now extend from Hungary to Turkey, from the Black Sea to the Adriatic and, some would say, all the way to Russia, central Asia and China; and a set of bubbling inter-ethnic links, albeit often underpinned with private violence and force, that criss-cross the Balkan's numerous political, communal and ethnified borders.

Explanations for this burgeoning transnational activity, which eludes official statistics, usually focus on the weakness of the state in the western Balkans—poorly controlled borders, lack of administrative capacity, power of organized crime, widespread corruption. In such accounts the state appears as the passive victim of the forces beyond its control, which can only be countered by the firm establishment of legal authority. In the words of Bulgarian political scientist, Ivan Krastev (2004), corruption and the accompanying ills have become the black myth of the post-communist transitions—countered, not surprisingly, by the rule of law as the 'magic phrase' that will bring in foreign investment, secure property rights and stimulate economic development.

This paper offers a slightly different interpretation of informal and illicit transnationalism in the Balkans. It is built around two interrelated arguments. First, by comparing contemporary patterns of illicit trade with the merchant-based economy of the late Ottoman Empire, I will try to show that the behaviour of Balkan merchants is neither historically unprecedented nor a deviation in the global economy. Rather, just as in the age of empires, Balkan merchants are resurrecting the old trade routes and, in the process, reconstituting the western Balkans as a dual periphery, simultaneously included and excluded from Europe, a part and parcel of the global economy but also its illicit counterpart. Second, following Giorgio Agamben's (1998; 2005) recent re-conceptualization of sovereignty—in which sovereign authority depends first and foremost on its ability to suspend law and create juridical zones of exception—I will argue that illicit activities in the Balkans have thrived and continue to thrive thanks to the chequered nature of the international state system, where areas of law and lawlessness tend to be mutually constituted and inextricably entwined. In other words, I will argue that the relationship between statehood and illicit trade in the modern world-economy is not conflictual (as, for instance, all the 'rule of law' arguments presume) but symbiotic. This interpretation of informal and illicit transnational forces thus questions some of the current policy prescriptions imposed on the Balkans—particularly the insistence on the rule of law as a panacea for all its economic woes. For, while the rule of law may encourage foreign capital to enter the Balkans (especially if the rule of law also implies institutional isomorphism with the EU), the further criminalization of local merchants and informal trade may, just as it did in the past, again curtail any possibility of local capital accumulation.

Resurrecting the Old Trade Routes

Ottoman rule in southeastern Europe, which lasted nearly five centuries, is usually considered as the period of great stagnation, if not outright decline, of the Balkans. The agricultural nature of the Ottoman economic system, the Empire's presumed voluntary exclusion from the thriving European world economy of the 15th–19th centuries, its expensive military establishment, and the total absence of an Industrial Revolution, kept the Balkans—or so it is argued—on the margins of both the European and Ottoman worlds. Expansion of the Austro-Hungarian Empire into southeastern Europe and the Serb and Greek wars of independence in the 19th century are thus regarded as the beginnings of the Balkans' re-inclusion in the civilized world and the European society of states.

Such a portrayal of this long period in Balkan history neglects the development of thriving merchant communities and the rapid urbanization of the region under the Ottomans (Fleat, 1999; Stoianovich, 1960). Several factors contributed to the development of trade in southeastern Europe between the 16th and 19th centuries. First, the Ottomans were keen to develop Istanbul into a commercial centre of the Levant and, for that reason, they fostered overland trade with the West in silk, sugar, spices and coffee. Second, Istanbul itself was dependent on the provision of goods—grain, salt, cattle, wool—from the Balkans. Hence the western provinces—Wallachia, Rumelia, Molodova and Bosnia—quickly became the main suppliers of the Ottoman capital. Third, the exclusion of non-Ottoman ships from the Black Sea (for security reasons) undermined the already weakened Genoese and Venetian traders in the Mediterranean, reinforced the privileged position of the Ragusans (from Dubrovnik, Ragusa being its earlier name) in the Adriatic, and encouraged the development of land routes across the Empire (Mirkovich, 1943; Stoianovich, 1960). Finally, wars in Europe and the increased demand for grain from the 18th century onwards expanded the boundaries of food supply chains deep into the Ottoman Empire and pushed and pulled Balkan peasants into trade with Europeans themselves (Kasaba, 1988).

Ottoman merchants, with the exception of traders who controlled eastern parts of the Empire, were rarely Turks or even Moslems. Throughout the Ottoman reign trade was mostly conducted by Greek, Armenian, Jewish, Serb or Ragusan merchants who settled in various parts of the Empire—or even further afield, in Hungary or Holland—and relied on the strength of their 'weak ties', familial, religious or ethnic, to carry it on. One group of merchants specialized in provision of the Ottoman capital with foods and necessities from the Balkans; the other traded in luxuries between Istanbul and Europe. On trade routes that spread throughout the Empire, linking Istanbul with the western provinces and the Hapsburgs, or Ragusa and Spalato in the south with the Danube in the north, emerged and thrived numerous new cities—Sarajevo, Skopje, Belgrade, Novi Pazar, Monastir, Larissa and Skadar, to name just a few (Stoianovich, 1960).

Travelling through the Balkan hinterlands of the Ottoman Empire in the late 17th century, famous Turkish travel-writer, Evliya Celebi (1996), described the city of Novi Pazar as a place situated on seven rivers with 3000 homes, nine water fountains,

23 mosques, two hamams, seven churches, 48 kinds of apples and 35 kinds of pears, 10 000 acres of vineyards and 1100 stores in the market. Founded in the 16th century, Novi Pazar (New Market)—or Yeni Pazar as it was known in the Ottoman Empire— rapidly grew into a key merchant centre in the Bosnian province, and one of the largest in the Balkans. At the time of the Austrian annexation of Bosnia, in the late 18th century, Novi Pazar remained a part of the Ottoman Empire, but not without contestation. Austrians, Serbs, Montenegrins and Ottomans all desired the Sandžak (Ottoman adminis- trative region) of Novi Pazar, and in 1908–09 the struggle between Austria and Russia over the Novi Pazar railway project, which was to link the Ottoman Empire with central Europe via the Sandžak, became the 'dress rehearsal' for the crisis of 1914 and the start of World War I (May, 1938). In 1912 the Sandžak was taken over by Serbian and Montenegrin troops, and split between the two kingdoms. In 1918, after World War I, it became part of the newly formed Kingdom of Serbs, Croats and Slovenians, predecessor of modern Yugoslavia. As Thomas Pynchon (1973, p.14) remarked, in one of the more enigmatic passages of *Gravity's Rainbow*, "on this obscure sanjak had once hinged the entire fate of Europe".

Throughout the rest of the 20th century, however, Sandžak—as the area became colloquially known—declined into oblivion. Disconnected from railways, and out of the way of any major routes to Europe, Sandžak's trading activities came to a halt. In a series of successive migrations, mostly to Turkey (in the aftermath of the two world wars in particular), the area was nearly depopulated. In 1945 Novi Pazar had fewer than 10 000 inhabitants. Industry never took off, and the city and the region were reduced to poverty. Even today, Sandžak is officially one of the least developed areas in Serbia and in Montenegro (six Sandžak cities—Novi Pazar, Tutin, Sjenica, Nova Varoš, Prijepolje and Priboj are in Serbia, five—Bijelo Polje, Rožaje, Plav, Pljevlja and Berane—in Montenegro). Tutin is the most underdeveloped city in Serbia, and the official unemployment rate in Novi Pazar is 33%. The population exodus from Sandžak continued through the 1990s, as the area's predominantly Muslim population, fearing persecution by Serbs and Montenegrins, departed for Bosnia and Herzegovina or Turkey and rejoined long lost family members (Biševac, 2001; ICG, 2005).

However, official statistics disguise the booms and busts of the informal economy in the area, and the critical role played by the Sandžak diaspora in that recovery. Starting with the 1980s, when the severe economic crisis in Yugoslavia and perpetual devaluations of the Yugoslav dinar put an end to informal trade with Italy and Austria (Trieste, in particular), suitcase traders turned to Istanbul as the source of cheap textiles and leather products, cosmetics, coffee and various household goods. The Sandžak diaspora assumed the role of intermediary in this trade, from organizing special bus lines to Istanbul to the actual purchase, shipment and distribution of goods from the Istanbul 'Balkan' market (where most shop owners were themselves originally from Sandžak) to open-air markets across the former Yugoslavia (Eder, 2004). In addition, the Sandžak diaspora controlled most of the underground market for foreign currency with networks of traders—often students or retired relatives—in most major Yugoslav cities. With the advent of the war in Bosnia, and the introduction of sanctions in Serbia, trade and trafficking of cigarettes, oil and alcohol through Sandžak accelerated as the region came to benefit from its geographically central position on the borders between Bosnia, Serbia and Montenegro.

At the same time Sandžak also became the manufacturing kingdom of counterfe it goods. A number of factories made fake packaging and labels for a range of products—from cigarettes such as Marlboro to the Croatian food additive Vegeta; many others engaged in production of counterfeit textiles (Levi's, Versace, Armani, Calvin Klein, Lacoste) and leather products (Louis Vuiton, Fendi, Prada). In the late 1990s it was estimated that Novi Pazar had at least 250 to 300 jeans factories, and probably just as many producing t-shirts, sweatshirts, sportswear and footwear (ICG, 2005). The area employed more than 10 000 people in textile manufacturing alone. Raw materials— fabric and yarn—were imported, mostly from Turkey, but also from Greece, Cyprus and Southern Italy through Montenegro, and trading was done exclusively in stable foreign currencies. The entire town of Novi Pazar, as one newspaper reporter noted, was "regarded as a big outlet store by factory and shop owners" (Perić-Zimonjić, 2001).

The Kosovo conflict of 1999 and the subsequent political changes in Serbia apparently shattered the economy of Novi Pazar. The loss of the Kosovo market, either because of the bombing and its aftermath or because of the uncertainties and dangers of the Kosovo situation after it came under UN protection, was coupled with the loss of Serbian and Montenegrin markets. The lifting of sanctions opened up borders and enabled shopkeepers from Serbia proper and Montenegro to make their purchases in Turkey without Sandžak intermediaries. Commerce was also hurt by the arrival of tens of thousands of Chinese traders in Serbia at the time of Milosevic's rule (Chinese markets now exist in most major Balkan cities). These traders started selling much cheaper Chinese goods in markets and in the streets, brought into Yugoslavia on daily Beijing–Belgrade flights or suitcased across the Russian–Hungarian trade route (ICG, 2005). The response of Sandžak entrepreneurs to the tightening of nearby markets has since been to reorient their exports towards the West (Germany in particular); meanwhile many smaller merchants have succumbed to pressure and sold their firms to large investors from Belgrade or Podgorica. Nevertheless, in comparison with the rest of Serbia, Novi Pazar continues to look like an economic miracle.

The story of Novi Pazar is not unique. Throughout the Balkans and across central and eastern Europe new/old market centres have emerged over the past decade. Perhaps the most famous market in Bosnia and Herzegovina is the so-called Arizona market, in the northeast, near Brčko. Brčko, which is now a unique political–economic district under the direct supervision of the Office of the High Representative (OHR), since its status is still disputed between the Serb and Muslim/Croat entities of post-Dayton Bosnia, was once also a major trading city. Most of the Bosnian trade in prunes—17.5% of its exports in late 1800s—went through Brčko). Arizona market (the name comes from that given by US peacekeepers to the route on which the market is situated) came into existence immediately after Dayton. It was fostered by the international peacekeeping forces as a way of encouraging inter-ethnic cooperation. What started off as a flea market, where small-scale vendors traded goods brought in bags from Hungary, Romania, Turkey or Bulgaria, has now grown into a 'merchant city' with over 2000 stands and between 20 000 and 40 000 customers per day.

In 2000 Arizona market changed hands—from a Croat-controlled municipality of Ravno Brčko to the District of Brčko, and the latter now collects over US$4 million in annual revenue (taxes and rent) from vendors. In 2002 the District Government revealed plans to further formalize the market and build it into an economic and merchants centre for southeastern Europe. To that effect, a contract was awarded to a local–Italian joint venture, 'Italproject', to transform Arizona market into a commercial paradise with more than 60 commercial facilities, a conference centre, multiplex cinemas, hotels and casinos. The project, now the largest construction site in southeastern Europe, is worth over $200 million, and it is expected that it will be completed by 2007. However, the prospects of enormous revenue as well as the disputed character of the Brčko District cause continuous conflicts between (predominantly Croat) landowners of the plots where Arizona is located, the representatives of the District Government and Italproject over land tenure (Showdown at Arizona Market, 2004). At the same time charges that Arizona is also a major women and drug trafficking centre abound, making the future of the project less certain than it would at first appear.

In the north of former Yugoslavia, in Subotica, on the border with Hungary, another flea market has already been transformed into a major commercial centre. 'Mali Bajmok', as the market is called, emerged at the end of the 1980s, when the first traders from Hungary, Poland, Romania, Bulgaria and the former Soviet Union started coming to former Yugoslavia. Initially the exchanges seemed almost surreal—Russians and eastern Europeans were mostly bringing antiques, communist paraphernalia and household junk, and then trading it for textiles and leather goods from Turkey, brought by Yugoslav (often Sandžak) merchants, that could later be resold on markets in their home countries. Most of the trade was barter, as money in these hyper-inflated economies was often virtually worthless, and it continued throughout the period of Yugoslav wars, despite (or perhaps thanks to) the sanctions imposed on Serbia. Today, 'Mali Bajmok' looks like a territorialized versi of E-bay with 1600 stands and more than 30 000 visitors per day. Not surprisingly, it also has an on-line version available at www.buvljak.info.

In the south of former Yugoslavia, on the borders between Montenegro and Albania, a small city called Tuza re-emerged in the 1990s as the main trafficking centre for oil, brought in at the border crossing in Rožaje. Tuza, once a caravan post for salt merchants, was transformed into a series of gas stations (reports say that nearly every house had a pump) and Montenegrins came in droves to fill their tanks there. In the latter part of the 1990s, the traffic of oil moved onto Lake Skadar, where it was transported—along with cigarettes, satellite dishes and electronic products—in small boats from Albania into Montenegro. Nearby areas thrived on this commerce, regaining their long forgotten historical importance (Ratković, 1994a; 1994b).

Finally, Istanbul has again become the key commercial centre for the entire region. Aside from the Grand Bazaar, which now includes concentric rings of merchants from Turkey, Persia, Afghanistan and central Asia, specialized markets for nearby countries have also emerged. Mine Eder (2002; 2003; 2004) has done research on Laleli district of Istanbul, which supplies markets in the former Soviet Union. The trade, which started in the early 1990s mostly as an individual suitcase business, is now increasingly formalized, with large cargo companies transporting goods from Laleli to Moscow, and the once-street vendors in Moscow acting as wholesalers/distributors of these goods to Russian regional markets. The already mentioned Balkan market, controlled by merchants from Sandžak, performs the same function for the territories of the former Yugoslavia. And, needless to say, Istanbul is also a deal-making centre for numerous illicit trade activities—from oil to drugs to human trafficking—as all the routes from Asia to Europe seem still to lead through the Bosphorus.

Thus, from Debrecen and Nyregyhaza in the northeastern corner of Hungary—where local markets (somewhat smaller than the one in Subotica though strikingly similar in physical appearance) attract and supply Ukranians, Romanians and assorted others (including Chinese) with goods from all over southeastern Europe—through numerous border towns in Bosnia and Herzegovina, Serbia, Montenegro and Croatia which thrive precisely on the basis of these multiple borders, and all the way down to Istanbul—the hub of Euro-Asian trade—contours of a different region than the one defined by the political and military mappings of states and armies are beginning to appear. Providing income and livelihood to hundreds of thousands of people, and enormous wealth to a few, commerce through southeastern Europe is now reconstituting the area as both distinct from and integrated into the world market economy.

Goods

Three kinds of goods, situated along the spectrum from legal and untaxed to uniformly illicit, cross the Balkan borders. In the first group are goods that can be found in the open markets described above—textiles, underwear, linen, shoes, counterfeit products, small household goods, plastic ware, construction material. Many of these are produced in sweatshops across the Balkans, such as the already described factories of Sandžak and Novi Pazar, or in textile factories in Bulgaria, Romania and Hungary. Just as many are brought from markets and merchants in Istanbul, and manufactured either in small establishments around Istanbul, Edirne, Izmir or Bursa or in the depths of Anatolia. Usually irregulars and discards intended for Western markets, these goods are clear signifiers of globally dispersed production and centralized distribution—the so-called buyer-driven commodity chains (Gereffi & Korzeniewicz, 1993). Made on order for large retailers such as Target, Wal-Mart, Gap, Guess or Esprit—and then deemed unsatisfactory or simply refused as surplus—the products find their way onto markets for a fraction of their cost in stores, and serve as the logical local counterpart to the malls and high-end retail outlets that are beginning to flourish in the region as well. The level of formalization of these markets varies from place to place, and from time to time, as does the importance of intermediaries. While suitcase trade continues to dominate, it is quite obvious that some of it is now conducted through large cargo shipments and with near-wholesaling scale of activities (Eder 2002; 2003).

The second type of good are stolen items—from items looted in wars, such as antiques and artwork or electronic products (TVs, VCRs, washing machines, computers, laptops) to cars. There are numerous car markets in southeastern Europe, but the one in Berkovići in Herzegovina is apparently one of the largest. Nested once again in a no-man's land between Eastern (Serb populated) and Western (Croat dominated) Herzegovina, close to Mostar (with a large Muslim population) and Montenegro, and en route to Croatia, Montenegro and Kosovo, the car market in Berkovići attracts miles of cars every weekend. Croats are the dealers, while Serbs and Montenegrins buy. Many vehicles have been stolen in western or eastern Europe (Hungary is, apparently, one of the most dangerous spots for foreign cars), or within the territories of former Yugoslavia itself. Refurbished with new licence plates and documentation, they disappear into markets in Kosovo or Macedonia and Albania. Benefiting from differences in customs duties between different states (and even entities) of former Yugoslavia, in lax border controls, and easy falsification of papers, dealers in stolen vehicles in Berkovići are the perfect intermediaries for organized crime networks throughout Europe.

The third type of good are illicit, high-profit items—oil, cigarettes, drugs and people. The schemes for their smuggling also vary. Oil, for instance has been smuggled throughout the past decade both by individuals and by large, state-owned or state-protected enterprises. As mentioned, it was carried in barrels on boats across Lake Skadar, and transported in the double tanks of individual cars across Montenegrin, Kosovan and Serbian borders. At one point, in the vicinity of Kula, another border-crossing town between Kosovo and Montenegro, smugglers even built a 10-mile long pipeline through the border zone, challenging both local and international authorities who, as expected, did nothing in response (Rexhepi, 2001a; 2001b).

But oil has also been a big state business. It is alleged that profits from oil smuggling and monopolies on its distribution financed the Bosnian Serbs throughout the war. Montenegro and Macedonia (via Thessaloniki), too, profited from sanctions against Serbia. Ports in the southern Adriatic and Aegean served as destinations for numerous oil tankers, the oil then being smuggled overland into Serbia, Bosnia or Kosovo. And speculations with oil continue—through the substitution of heating oil (which is tax-free in most parts of former Yugoslavia) for diesel, preferential grant of import licences, skewed distribution networks, and the development of politically protected monopolies and oligopolies (Karup-Druško, 2000).

Drug trafficking in southeastern Europe has now—allegedly—fallen mostly into the hands of Albanians. Again, it is widely believed, though just as much contested by Albanian patriots, that the drug trade through the Balkans financed most of the operations of the Kosovo Liberation Army before and in the aftermath of NATO bombing. Previously transported through former Yugoslavia, and then to Austria and Germany, because of the war drug trafficking was re-routed to Italy through Bulgaria, Macedonia and Albania. This has strengthened the role of Albanian traffickers; it is now estimated that the Balkan route accounts for some 80% of heroin destined for Europe (Cilluffo & Salmoiraghi, 1999).

Human smuggling through the Balkans has also become an extremely lucrative enterprise. The trafficking of women has attracted the most attention though, unfortunately, to no avail. According to UNDP data, more than 10 000 women passed through the Bijeljina-Brčko (Arizona Market)–Croatian border route in 2001 alone. There are also strong correlations between the presence of international peacekeepers and prostitution, if not trafficking itself (HRW, 2002; Lindstrom 2004; Mendelson, 2005). But over the past few years the smuggling of Chinese, Kurdish, Iranian, Jordanian and other Asian and Middle Eastern citizens through Macedonia, Kosovo, Serbia and Bosnia and Herzegovina seems to be achieving even greater proportions. The smugglers frequently take advantage of the total ignorance of the area by their human cargo, leaving them in fields in Serbia or Bosnia and claiming that they have been taken to Western Europe. Numerous tragic incidents and deaths involving illegal migrants have been reported throughout the region.

However, perhaps the least tragic but certainly the most significant branch of illicit trade in terms of volume and revenue has been the cigarette smuggling business. It can safely be said that the governments of Montenegro, Serbia, Croatia and Macedonia, and to a lesser degree of the Bosnian entities (particularly Republika Srpska), have been financing their activities from the tobacco trade since the beginning of the war in former Yugoslavia. There were two distinct strategies employed in this trade. The first was the production of counterfeit cigarettes, where domestic tobacco was used in local factories to produce fake major-label cigarettes (Dunhill, Rothmans, Marlboro). Given the number of tobacco growers (and the quality of Macedonian and Herzegovinian tobacco), as well as the number of cigarette making factories in the former Yugoslavia, one could have expected the counterfeit business to flourish, both in domestic war-torn markets and as an export. Instead, with a few notable exceptions (Tobacco Industry in Rovinj, Croatia and the Sarajevo Tobacco Factory, Bosnia and Herzegovina) most cigarette makers went out of business and tobacco growers continue to struggle. The second strategy—smuggling of imported, genuine-label cigarettes—proved far more profitable.

The most elaborate cigarette smuggling scheme was devised by the Montenegrins with the full consent and protection of Milo Djukanović's government. Cigarettes came into Montenegro either by planes from Rotterdam (some estimate that planes with 20–40 tons of cigarettes were flying into Podgorica, capital of Montenegro, every night for several years) or by boat through the ports of Bar and Ulcinj. From Montenegro cigarettes could go in two different directions. One lot was intended for the markets of former Yugoslavia (Serbia, Kosovo, Macedonia, Bosnia), where smuggled cigarettes would be sold on streets and in stores either without excise tax and label or with a fake label. The second lot would be transported by speedboat into Italy, and then back into Western Europe (Hozić, 2004).

While the scale of Montenegrin operations is fascinating, the scheme was not unique. Hard evidence is still lacking (although some law suits have been attempted), but there are indications that behind this complex passage of cigarettes through states such as Montenegro, Macedonia, or Croatia stand the world's largest tobacco industries— British American Tobacco, Philip Morris, RJ Reynolds. Faced with shrinking markets in Western Europe and the USA as a result of health regulations and extremely high taxes, tobacco majors are trying to recapture their share of customers by dumping cigarettes on states such as Montenegro, Andorra or Cyprus, from which they can relatively easily re-enter western Europe—but this time without taxes or duties. The advantage of the Balkan states—as opposed, for instance, to Andorra—is that they also have large markets themselves, and that smuggling cigarettes through their borders becomes a win-win proposition.

The Significance of Balkan Trade Routes Today

Several important parallels with the contemporary Balkans can be drawn from this brief detour into the past. First, the peculiarities of the Ottoman Empire—its division into a number of customs zones with different levels of import and export duties, different taxation scales for sea and overland trade, strict regulation of internal trade and prohibition of exports of provisionary staples to Europe—created, perhaps ironically, numerous opportunities for arbitrage, speculation and contraband trade. In short, they created an environment in which commerce could flourish. Thus, despite all its flaws, most importantly its ever-enlarging fiscal deficit, the Ottoman Empire proved to be an ideal place for the 'conquering Balkan Orthodox merchant' who successfully captured the trade between central Europe, Russia and the Ottoman Empire itself.

Second, the Balkans' peripheral position *vis-à-vis* both Europe and the Ottoman Empire made it ever more significant to both Europeans and the Ottomans. Southeastern Europe became the principal conduit in the reluctant mutual courtship and perpetual contest between the two worlds. Being situated in this double periphery allowed the Balkans to emerge as a peculiar self-enclosed zone through which only the initiated, the well acquainted, the domesticated could travel. Various forms of banditry—those of the uskoks of Senj to the hajduks of Serbia to Albanian and Montenegrin gangs—threatened foreign merchants and kept them, for the most part, off the Balkan overland routes. Thus the disorder, anarchy and danger associated with overland trade only further empowered the native Balkan merchants, eliminated their competition, and led to the formation of mini-merchant fiefdoms with their own protection forces and localized forms of authority.

Finally, the agricultural/military foundation of the Ottoman Empire, which exclusively favoured Muslims, left trade in the hands of foreigners or its non-Muslim population. Diasporas and migrations within the Balkans but also into Europe and Istanbul created natural bridges for merchants and allowed trade to flow through families, friendships, ethnic or village ties, without any major misgivings about trust or future exchanges. In addition, the Ottoman Empire also constituted the Balkans into a complex web of overlapping communities for whom the bounds of a nation-state could never fit. Trade flourished for those and among those who knew how to navigate the terrain of cultural difference; it antagonized those whose interests were first and foremost territorial—landowners and peasants, bureaucrats and their tax-paying subjects, foreigners and natives.

The contemporary Balkans—though not a part of a vast agricultural/militarized empire—exhibits many of these traits. Multiple borders (Bosnia alone has, at one point, had more than 400 border-crossings), different taxation systems, numerous refugee and diasporic communities all create a set of relations both within the Balkans, and between the Balkans, Europe and Turkey which seem exceptionally conducive to informal and illicit (contraband) trade. The Yugoslav wars, ironically, have not only disseminated arms throughout the region and perpetuated warlordism and private armies but have also recreated the image of the region as a dangerous, non-navigable space for outsiders. The presence of legions of global governance missionaries does not really change this picture. On the contrary, the foreigners create their own islands of sovereignty and tax-exemptions around which informal and illicit commerce can flourish, while their dependence on local interpreters (language and otherwise) creates yet another layer of intermediaries between the formal and informal economy.

The most important aspect of the re-emergence of the Balkan trade routes, however, rests precisely in the fact that they reconstitute the Balkans as a dual periphery, simultaneously included in and excluded from Europe, a part and parcel of the global economy and its illicit counterpart. The Balkans, as the example of goods traded in the area—cigarettes, oil and textiles in particular—now clearly shows, serves as a giant, semi-regulated (or at least often government-protected) off-shore territory where products that would otherwise have difficulty entering European or Western markets get recycled, laundered or refurbished, and then brought (back) into the West. Similarly to off-shore tax havens, recently described by Ronen Palan (2002), the Balkan states act like "parking lot proprietors: they could not care less about the business of their customers, only that they pay for parking their vehicles there" (Palan, 2002, p. 152). They offer protection services and local hideouts to global merchant corporations or organized crime networks, and help them create additional spaces of circulation for their goods without questioning their origin or worrying about their final destination.

The question of sovereignty, of the Balkan states' neither-here-nor-there position in Europe, then raises the issue of the Balkans anomaly—to what degree, if at all, are the Balkans an area of deviant lawlessness, corruption and crime? Palan's (2002) argument about tax havens seems quite pertinent to this question. The commercialization of sovereignty—the sale of sovereign space in exchange for the provision of protection services, anonymity and evasion of taxes—is not, in his view, just a simple response to the increased regulation and levels of taxation in advanced industrial countries. Rather, Palan argues, the commercialization of sovereignty is a pragmatic solution to an inherent contradiction between a state's increasing insulation in law, on the one hand, and the internationalization of capital (particularly via multinational corporations), on the other. The key to this solution is an element of juridical fiction rather than fact—the strategy of tax havens is based upon the premise that legal entities can establish a presence in their territories without actually relocating. Thus, says Palan, not only are tax havens and their "prostitution of sovereign rights", endemic to the state system, they are also constitutive of a "virtual state system" that feeds off the juridical and political infrastructure of the "real" state system and enables the smooth functioning of the global economy (Palan, 2002; 2003).

James Mittelman and Robert Johnston (1999) offer a similar analysis of the relationship between states and organized crime. The emerging 'courtesan state', as they call it (analogies to prostitution in both analyses are quite interesting in themselves), finds itself in a subservient position to the more powerful interests in the global political economy and, while offering services to its wealthy clients, advanced industrial countries, it neglects the provision of social services for its underclass. Organized crime steps into this void and acts as an intermediary between the two worlds. Therefore, according to Mittelman and Johnston, organized crime can be seen as a manifestation of a Polanyian double movement, the consequence of an expanding global economy and the search for forms of social protection.

What both of these analyses share is a sense that the clash between economic liberalization and the state's embeddedness in a set of laws generates its own perversions which, in turn, allow the global economic system to continue to function. The best example of an endemic and deviant state in the Balkans may be Bosnia and Herzegovina, entirely a construct of the international community and liberal economic order. The international community insists on those attributes of statehood that will enable international capital to flow freely through Bosnia and Herzegovina (e.g. standardization of business regulations and taxation regimes with advanced industrial countries, allowing global merchants to operate there just as easily as in Singapore). However, local merchants continue to maintain internal barriers and legal idiosyncrasies which strengthen their own position. As a result, the state operates as a no-man's land, combining elements of both legality and illegality in which informal markets and illicit trade—as a way of connecting Bosnia and Herzegovina to world markets—continue to thrive.

But there is another element of these analyses worth mentioning. What both Palan and Mittelman and Johnston emphasize is that sovereign exceptions are endogenous to the international state system; and that lawlessness (or the prostitution of law, in their terminology) is part and parcel of the contemporary global economy. In this they come close to Giorgio Agamben's (1998) works on sovereignty, which also emphasize that it is the exception and not the law which constitutes the essence of sovereign power. I have described elsewhere (Hozić, 2002) how media representation of the Balkans over the past 10 years or so has helped construe it into precisely such a zone of sovereign exception as to make the extant sovereign order possible. Here it would suffice to say that that such a politics of representation has had its counterpart in actual economic flows. The Balkans, as the alleged zone of lawlessness and corruption, may indeed be an integral part of the world economy, sustaining the functioning of the international state system rather than eroding it.

Conclusion: The World of Merchants

A few final remarks must be made about the world construed by global and local merchants and the emergence of the old trade routes. Over the past two decades the character of global capitalism has dramatically altered. The predominant form of corporate organization are now large wholesalers—companies whose production is dispersed around the world but whose branding, marketing and distribution are nonetheless centralized. The new buyer-driven commodity chains (Gereffi & Korzeniewicz, 1993) are governed and ruled by merchants and/or providers of financial services in both exporting and importing countries. Their primary interest, for years, has been the unobstructed mobility of capital and production in search of the most advantageous—tax-wise and labour-wise— environments. Far less concerned with political stability and order than traditional manu-facturers, these global corporate merchants have both stimulated the development of and thrived on the contradictions between economic liberalization and sovereignty. As a result, the zones of sovereign exception—tax havens, pirate states, failed states, states of lawlessness, 'courtesan' states—have proliferated.

In all such spaces—and the Balkans is just one of them, although the size of its market and its location make it particularly important—local merchant networks have also emerged. Local merchants (whose relationship with statehood, as mentioned in the case of Bosnia and Herzegovina, may be quite different from the relationship of global merchants) act as intermediaries not just between geographic locations otherwise inaccessible to global merchants, but also between different legal and cultural environ-ments, capitalizing on the danger associated with their trade. The outcome is a complex web of roads and territories, multiple forms of sovereignty, private protection forces, and thriving—or desperate—diasporas.

However, the process of informal transnationalization is not irreversible. It is worth noting that the end to the thriving Balkan commerce came precisely at the time when the Balkans was reintegrated into the European economy and increasingly distanced from its Ottoman centre (Inalcik & Quataert,1994; Palairet, 1997). The four newly inde-pendent states which emerged from the Congress of Berlin—Serbia, Bulgaria, Greece and Romania—all attempted to 'modernize', but such initiative, in the words of John Lampe, often "derived from noneconomic motives and discouraged growth" (Lampe & Jackson, 1982, p. 157). Industry was slow to develop and trade, in particular, suffered. Ironically, the states which were, for the most part, formed as a result of desire by their wealthy merchants to capture the entirety of export profits, without paying any additional tribute to the Ottomans, could no longer generate their once customary export surpluses, either because of the protectionist measures of their northern neighbour, the Austro-Hungarian Empire, or because production on their own soil could not compare with the richness and vastness of the area that they could draw on in the days of the Ottoman trade. Parts of the Balkans that remained within the Ottoman Empire—the Sandžak of Novi Pazar, Albania, Macedonia, Thrace—suffered even more. Cut off from their European markets, and confronted by the shrinking and increasingly unstable Istanbul market, the European territories of the Ottoman Empire declined into near oblivion.

The lands which were under the control of the Hapsburgs fared only slightly better. Slovenia's and Croatia's integration into Central European markets allowed trade to continue through their territories. But their industries could hardly compete with far more developed Czech and Austrian producers, and their agriculture lagged behind the large-scale agricultural production in Hungary (Lampe & Jackson, 1982). Bosnia, however, became the paradigmatic case of a state that lost its entire merchant class because of its integration into the Hapsburg Empire. In 1879, following Austrian occupation, Bosnia and Herzegovina became a part of the customs territory of Austria-Hungary. This meant that the Hapsburg law on customs and monopolies—and state monopolies in the Austro-Hungarian Empire included gunpowder, salt and tobacco, while excise taxes were levied on brandy and sugar—was extended to Bosnia. The law literally ruined Bosnian merchants, whose major wholesaling business had previously been precisely in salt and tobacco. In addition, the customs provisions of the law cut them off from their main trading partner, the Ottoman Empire. The combination of monopolies and customs, coupled with the haphazard railway construction, which pitted Austrian and Hungarian interests in the province against each other but totally neglected those of the Bosnians, practically disconnected Bosnia and Herzegovina from any of its possible export markets while making it hostage to the needs of the Hapsburg Empire (Sugar, 1963).

The end to Balkan trade in the days of the Ottoman Empire, therefore, came with its accession to the European society of states. At a time when Bosnia and Herzegovina and Kosovo remain the last states with an unresolved status and relation to the European Union, the provocative question with which to end this paper is, perhaps: is the memory of this exclusion, currently revived in the numerous flea markets and contraband trade, more worth preserving than the prospect of accession to the European Union?

References

Agamben, G. (1998) *Homo Sacer: Sovereign Power and Bare Life*, trans. Daniel Heller-Roazen (Stanford, CA: Stanford University Press).

Agamben, G. (2005) *State of Exception*, trans. Kevin Attell (Chicago, IL: University of Chicago Press).

Andreas, P. (2004) The clandestine political economy of war and peace in Bosnia, *International Studies Quarterly*, 48, pp. 29–51.

Andreas, P. (2005) Criminalizing consequences of sanctions: embargo busting and its legacy, *International Studies Quarterly*, 49, pp. 335–360.

Athanassopoulou, E. (2004) Introduction: fighting organised crime in SEE, *Southeast European and Black Sea Studies*, 4(2), pp. 217–222.

Biševac, S. (2000) Bosniaks in Sandžak and interethnic tolerance in Novi Pazar, in: N. Dimitrijević (Ed.), *Managing Multiethnic Local Communities in the Countries of the Former Yugoslavia* (Budapest: Local Government and Public Service Reform Initiative).

Bojičić, V. & Kaldor, M. (1999) The 'abnormal' economy of Bosnia-Herzegovina, in: C. Schierup (Ed.), *Scramble for the Balkans*, pp. 92–117 (New York: St. Martin Press).

Celebi, E. (1996) *Putopis: odlomci o jugoslovenskim zemljama* (Sarajevo: Sarajevo Publishing).

Cilluffo, F.J. & Salmoiraghi, G. (1999) And the winner is...Albanian mafia, *Washington Quarterly*, 22(4), pp. 21–25.

Eder, M. with Carkoglu, A., Yakovlev, A. & Chaudry, K. (2002) Redefining contagion: the political economy of suitcase trade between Turkey and Russia, International Research & Exchanges Board (IREX) Wasington DC, Black Sea and Caspian Sea Project, unpublished report.

Eder, M. (2003) From suitcase trade to organized informal trade? The case of Laleli district in Istanbul, paper presented at the Fourth Mediterranean Social and Political Research Meeting, Robert Schuman Center for Advanced Studies part of the European University Institute in Florence, Italy.

Eder, M. (2004) Istanbul as a city of merchants: a case of transnationalism from below, paper presented at the International Studies Association Annual Meeting, Montreal.

Fleat, K. (1999) *European and Islamic Trade in the Early Ottoman State: The Merchants of Genoa and Turkey* (Cambridge: Cambridge University Press).

Gereffi, G. & Korzeniewicz, M. (Eds) (1993) *Commodity Chains and Global Capitalism* (Wesport, Connecticut: Greenwood Press).

Government Accounting Office (2000) Bosnia peace operation: crime and corruption threaten successful implementation of the Dayton Peace Agreement, Testimony, 19 July 2000, GAO/T-NSIAD 00-219, available online at: http://www.fas.org/man/gao/nsiad-00-219.htm.

Hajdinjak, M. (2002) *Smuggling in Southeast Europe: The Yugoslav Wars and the Development of Regional Criminal Networks in the Balkans* (Sofia: Center for the Study of Democracy).

Hozić, A. (2002) Zoning: or how to govern (cultural) violence?, *Cultural Values*, 6(1), pp. 183–195.

Hozić, A. (2004) Between the cracks: Balkan cigarette smuggling, *Problems of Post-Communism*, 51(3), pp. 35–44.

Human Rights Watch (HRW) (2002) Hopes betrayed: trafficking of women and girls to post-conflict Bosnia and Herzegovina for forced prostitution, *Human Rights Watch Report*, 14(9).

International Crisis Group (ICG) (2005) *Serbia's Sandzak: Still Forgotten*, Europe Report 162 (Brussels: ICG).

Inalcik, H. & Quataert, D. (1994) *An Economic and Social History of the Ottoman Empire 1300–1914* (Cambridge: Cambridge University Press).

Jung, D. (Ed.) (2003) *Shadow Globalization, Ethnic Conflicts, and New Wars: A Political Economy of Intrastate Wars* (London: Routledge).

Karup-Druško, Dž. (2000) Šema naftne mafije, *Naši Dani*, 178, 27 October.

Kasaba, R. (1988) *The Ottoman Empire and the World Economy* (Albany, NY: SUNY Press).

Krastev, I. (2004) *Shifting Obsessions: Three Essays on the Politics of Anticorruption* (Budapest: CEU Press).

Lampe, J. & Jackson, M. (1982) *Balkan Economic History, 1550–1950: From Imperial Borderlands to Developing Nations* (Bloomington, IN: Indiana University Press).

Lindstrom, N. (2004) Regional sex trafficking in the Balkans: transnational networks in the enlarged Europe, *Problems of Post-Communism*, 51(3), pp. 45–52.

May, A.J. (1938) The Novibazar railway project, *Journal of Modern History*, 10(4), pp. 496–527.

Mendelson, S.E. (2005) Barracks and brothels: peacekeeping and human trafficking in the Balkans (Washington, DC: The CSIS Press).

Mirkovich, N. (1943) Ragusa and the Portuguese spice trade, *Slavonic and East European Review: American Series*, 2(1), pp. 174–187.

Mittelman, J. & Johnston, R. (1999) The globalization of organized crime: the courtesan state, and the corruption of civil society, *Global Governance*, 5(1), pp.103–127.

Palairet, M. (1997) *The Balkan Economies c. 1800–1914: Evolution Without Development* (Cambridge: Cambridge University Press).

Palan, R. (2002) Tax havens and the commercialization of state sovereignty, *International Organization*, 56(1), pp. 151–176.

Palan, R. (2003) *The Offshore World* (Ithaca, NY: Cornell University Press).

Perić-Zimonjić, V. (2001) Economy: an island of prosperity and tolerance in Serbia, *IPS News*, 3 September.

Pugh, M. (2002) Postwar political economy in Bosnia and Herzegovina: the spoils of peace, *Global Governance*, 8, pp. 467–482.

Pugh, M. (2004) Rubbing salt into war wounds: shadow economies and peacebuilding in Bosnia and Kosovo, *Problems of Post-Communism*, 51(3), pp. 53–61.

Pynchon, T. (1973) *Gravity's Rainbow* (New York: Viking Press).

Ratković, M. (1994a) Nafta ili voda, AIM Press Podgorica, 1 July, available online at: http://www.aimpress.org/dyn/pubs/archive/data/199407/40701-002-pubs-pod.html.

Ratković, M. (1994b) Nafta ili voda: Skadarsko jezero izmedju ekologije i politike, 1 July, available online at: http://www.aimpress.or/dyn/pubs/archive/data/199407/40701-002-pubs-pri.htm.

Rexhepi, I. (2001a) Naftovod koji nikome ne smeta, AIM Press Priština, 30 November, available online at: http://www.aimpress.org/dyn/pubs/archive/data/200112/11201-003-pubs-pri.htm.

Rexhepi, I. (2001b) Naftovod koji nikome ne smeta, AIM Press Priština, 11 November, available at online at: http://www.aimpress.or/dyn/pubs/archive/data/200112/11201-003-pubs-pri.htm.

Showdown at Arizona Market (2004) Investigative journalism project funded by IREX, available online at: http://www.dicar.dk/files/artikler/art237.htm.

Stoianovich, T. (1960) The conquering Balkan Orthodox merchant, *Journal of Economic History*, 20(1), pp. 234–313.

Sugar, P. (1963) *Industrialization of Bosnia-Hercegovina 1878–1918* (Seattle, WA: University of Washington Press).

Transnationalization of Civil Society in Kosovo: International and Local Limits of Peace and Multiculturalism

ANA DEVIC

This paper sets out to outline the political relevance of a highly prioritized goal of foreign assistance in Kosovo: the development of a non-governmental sector in charge of peace building and what is customarily termed 'multi-ethnic coexistence' or 'multiculturalism'. Given the practical situation on the ground six years after the setting-up of the UN protectorate in Kosovo—a nearly complete individual and institutional segregation between Kosovan Albanians and Serbs—I seek to explain why the foreign-assisted and evidently increasingly transnationalizing (or Westernizing) civil society sector has not so far developed any significant leverage against the dominance of ethno-nationalist divisions in Kosovo. The most striking observation of this study is that the dramatic increase in the number of civil society-building non-governmental organizations (NGOs), subscribing, in both their proclaimed general goals and in their individual projects' objectives, to a multi-ethnic Kosovo, has not contributed to a more sustained involvement of ordinary Kosovans in civil society activities. Nor has there been a sustained impact on the part of civil society NGOs on the political reality of the UN protectorate.

I begin with a discussion of the definitions and practices of civil society in the region and in Kosovo in particular. I then move on to summarize and interpret findings and observations from a number of surveys with the goal of support or objecting to the initial theses on the problems of a foreign-aided civil society in Kosovo *vis-à-vis* the goals of peace and multiculturalism. I argue that an incomplete analysis and knowledge on the part of Western aid organizations of the local civil society in Kosovo before 1999 has simultaneously contributed to the marginalization of many pre-existing civil society organizations and to the over-estimation of what a brand new internationally funded civil society can actually accomplish in the face of powerful political pressures stemming from the zero-sum game of Kosovan prospective state sovereignty (or its denial). In other words, Western actors have neglected the effect that deep political fissures, i.e. mutually exclusive state-building agendas, have had upon a previously politicized and forcibly ethnically segregated civil society. Further, I will demonstrate that civil society actors take enormous risks when questioning the moral and social legitimacy of ethnocentric state building, which may have little to do with local everyday-life practices of inter-ethnic relations, but quite a lot to do with NGO allegiance to ethno-centred definitions of the Kosovo statehood. In several ways, ironically, Kosovan NGO-ized civil society faces greater pressure from Western donors and mediators to implement peace building and multiculturalism than do the Kosovan political elites.

The paper follows the political opportunity structure approach (e.g. Tarrow, 1998), which is deemed far more helpful than the popular historicist–nationalist view of ethnic segregation in Kosovo for understanding why ethno-centred nationalist political agendas are still preferred by a great number of civil society groups as more reliable and safe 'master frames' of their relationship with Kosovan political elites. Simultaneously the same civic actors are well positioned in the transnational international aid industry: they incorporate the goals of a 'multi-ethnic Kosovo' in their projects' ideological universe. Finally, I will propose that plans for a transnational or Western-style multiculturalism—as a social and political programme that would stabilize Kosovo regardless of its future status—may inadvertently perpetuate the nationalist, i.e. ethno-centred state-building agenda, as in post-Dayton Bosnia and Herzegovina. I argue that the sort of multiculturalism that draws on the Western model of integration of minorities or immigrants in terms of 'majority-being-sensitive-to-minority' instantly demonstrates—in post-violence and state status-pending Kosovo—the ultimate 'nuisance' that the sheer multiple presence of minorities (Serbs in south-central Kosovo, Albanians in the Serb-controlled north, Roma everywhere) creates for the majority-centred concept of state building, which, in Kosovo, is still to be approved (or denied).

The Record of Local Civil Society

There is a broad consensus that a vibrant civil society is an essential component of any robust democratic infrastructure, and that reversing its relative weakness in Kosovo is vital for the establishment of a sustainable peace. So far this function has largely been carried out through the efforts of international organizations, which arrived at once and in large numbers following the 1999 NATO intervention, landing among local civic and political actors that had for long suffered from the deleterious impact of political violence, discrimination and isolation.

Kosovan civil society developed during the 1990s in the form of 'parallel structures', offering educational and health services to those whose access to government provision was impaired as a result of ethno-political discrimination. It also contributed, albeit to a lesser degree, to the development of awareness concerning human rights and gender issues. The majority of underground civil society activists were Kosovo Albanian professionals who during the late1980s and mid-1990s were dismissed from their jobs in state schools, universities, courts and hospitals, and replaced with Serbs. From 1988 ethnic apartheid was gradually institutionalized as the rise of Slobodan Milošević to power in the Serbian League of Communists was marked by the abolition of the constitutional autonomy of the two Serbian provinces (Kosovo and Vojvodina). It seems reasonable to ask why, in the aftermath of the 1999 military intervention and the establishment of the rule of theUnited Nations Mission in Kosovo (UNMIK), the 'parallel structures' did not become the foundation and the most valuable resource of the new internationally funded civil society? Answering this question requires a closer examination of pre-1999 civil society in Kosovo.

It is instructive to mention here the definitions of civil society that were upheld by local activists in Eastern Europe before 1989, since they also to some extent informed the ideology and practice of Kosovan 'parallel structures' during the 1990s. Civil society was regarded as a political project, to be carried out by informal groups who created opportunities for 'learning solidarity' beyond state control. In the famous formulation of George Konrad, 'antipolitics' (as synonymous with civil society of the time) was meant to hollow out the space of influence of the totalitarian state and prepare the ground for democratic development in the region (Konrad, 1984). Kosovan 'parallel structures' resembled the 'antipolitics' model to the extent that they operated entirely outwith Serbian state institutions, while the latter tacitly welcomed the fact that they took over nearly the entire sphere of social services provision for the Kosovo Albanian population. While in their earlier period the parallel structures espoused broader goals of democratic and social development, in their later stages the movement became focused on the struggle for Kosovo's independence from Yugoslavia and Serbia. This dynamic resulted from the increasing repression of the civilian population throughout the 1990s, which emptied all official institutions of Kosovo Albanians, while making it increasingly difficult to recruit qualified professionals into the ranks of the parallel structures (Maliqi, 1996). In this way, pressures to survive and resist the Serbian regime overshadowed the initial drive towards the democratization and pluralization of Kosovo, making the movement more rigid and autarkic by default, and increasingly delegitimized by the growing popular appeal of the plan for the violent ending of the Serbian oppression. Once the Serbian regime was driven out by the military campaigns of the Kosovo Liberation Army (KLA) and NATO, much of the entitlements of the parallel structures, whose many activities were previously supported by the solidarity funds collected from the Kosovo Albanian diaspora community, started to lose their rationale. In addition, and not surprisingly, a great number of former activists of the 'parallel structures was absorbed into the new Kosovo Albanian political parties and, later, into the institutions of provisional government. Partisan politics became the main investment in and agenda of public organizing, where the majority of younger leaders built their political capital not on the legacies of civic resistance, but on the success of their military campaigns and of their ultimate goal—state sovereignty.

During the 1990s the Kosovo Albanian system of parallel political institutions was coordinated by the League for Democratic Kosovo (LDK), founded in 1989, and led by the president in exile Ibrahim Rugova. The LDK based its mobilizational strategies on the pre-existing organizations of the Province's League of Communists, such as trades unions, and, especially in the rural areas, on a combination of the socialist-era and traditional patriarchal forms of authority and solidarity. Already in 1989 the LDK-led parallel structures had branched out into civil society voluntary associations, such as the Mother Teresa Society (still one of the largest local NGOs) and the Council for the Defence of Human Rights and Freedoms (CDHRF). Other organizations established at this time included women's and youth groups, as well as the Kosovo Helsinki Council. Most of these early civil society groups were founded by the CDHRF, and operated as a social welfare system of the government led by the LDK. The CDHRF is still very active in Kosovo, and closely cooperates with the larger international NGO partners such as Amnesty International, the International Federation of Human Rights, and the International Crisis Group.

To sum up, during the 1990s Kosovo Albanian civil society developed its grassroots base and dense activities across the province. However, these organizations were not natural predecessors of the post-1999 NGOs: on the one hand, they were almost exclusively oriented toward service provision, while, on the other, they operated in the context of enforced ethnic apartheid and a growing no-dissent-considered consensus about the goal of Kosovo independence. Although from time to time they reached agreement with the Serbian government in Belgrade concerning the use of hospitals in Serbia, they were not normally involved in any cooperative or advocacy work with or against the Serbian government. This is hardly surprising given the fact that these developments were taken place before the demise of the one-party political system in socialist Yugoslavia. Thus, Kosovo Albanian civil society groups were akin to semi-underground social movement organizations subordinated in their ideological and practical agenda to the 'shadow government' of the LDK (Nietsch, 2004, makes similar observations).

Civil Society Since 1999: the Parallel De-politicization and Transnationalization of the NGO Universe

Immediately after the war new NGOs mushroomed in Kosovo because of the sudden influx of international donor funding. Since 2002–03, when the humanitarian relief stage gave way to the stage of development, and when a large number of major donors started phasing out their operations, local NGOs have been faced with difficult and often contradictory options: to change their focus and specialization and adapt to yet another set of (new) donors' priorities, or to insist on their own perceptions of the priorities and needs of their direct beneficiaries and the wider population (Nietsch, 2004). In all cases they had to start competing for funding in a shrinking donors' market, or joining forces with other local NGOs to form larger more durable NGO networks. Their choices and space for manoeuvre were aggravated by a number of rules imposed by donors and large international NGO partners. Based on the examples that I will present below, it is possible to argue that, while the acceptance of internationally agreed and uniform definitions of peace and multi-ethnicity may have led to the better incorporation of Kosovan NGOs in the transnational flows and networks of the aid industry, such a process simultaneously hampers the long-term commitment and contribution of the local civil society to the development of political dimensions and institutions of multi- or inter-ethnic reality in Kosovo. The lack of political commitment of local NGOs to their stated goals of lasting peace building and its priorities is most strikingly manifested in the area of 'minority (Serb and Roma) returns'.

In the aftermath of the 1999 military intervention the most widespread practice pursued by the largest foreign aid donors in developing civil society in Kosovo was to create local NGOs as divisions of large international NGOs (Nietsch, 2004). More significant problems of autonomy of local NGOs, pertaining to priorities and methods of peace building, can be defined as problems of unequal 'partnership' with international actors. The same problem can be also said to affect NGOs' relationship with local elites, i.e. with the Provisional Institutions of Self-Government (PISG).[1] While 'partnership' seems to include a wide array of relationships, ranging from local NGOs being in sole charge of applying ideas of peace and multi-ethnicity that originate outside Kosovo to including creative input on the part of locals, most arrangements, in reality, fall into the category of 'instrumental' partnerships.[2] Here local actors are recognized as indispensable in implementing and operationalizing peace-building programmes, but are not considered equal partners in terms of offering their own definitions of problems and methods of dealing with them (White, 1996; see also in Llamazares & Reynolds Levy, 2003).

The imposition of the donors' definitions of peace and multi-ethnic justice had a more lasting negative effect in terms of neglecting both the local dynamics of inter-ethnic coexistence before 1999 and the post-1999 ethnic 'un-mixing' and out-migration trends. Examples of this neglect abound in the area of minority persons return, which is otherwise a highly prioritized goal. While nearly all programmes of international assistance focus on the 65 000 Roma and Serb internally displaced persons (IDPs) currently residing in the northern municipalities of Kosovo controlled by Serbian authorities, the reintegration of 130 000 Serbs still remaining in local political and social institutions in the rural 'enclaves' in southern Kosovo has not been prioritized.[3] Meanwhile, in some areas with mixed or 'enclaved' populations in central Kosovo, such as Prizren and Gjilan/Gnjilane, there have been significant improvements in multi-ethnic relations: mixed private schools and kindergartens are now popular (and profitable for their owners). During 2004 the fact that it was precisely in towns such as Prizren and Gjilan/Gnjilane that inter-ethnic relationships received some of the heaviest blows presents international actors with another unlearned lesson: minorities in the southern part of Kosovo were left outside the universe of multi-ethnic peace and reintegration programmes for nearly five years, while all energy and imagination was focused on the IDPs in Serbia and their prospects of return. Comparison between various interviews with IDPs in Serbia and with Serbs in the enclaves, as well as with local NGO personnel, reveals some sociological facts that international actors have barely considered when recommending the transnationally certified methods of 'minority return' as part of peace-building and multi-ethnicity agendas. A large number of Serb IDPs currently residing in Serbia are of urban origin and currently have greater prospects of finding jobs in Serbia, and their partial or 'limited' return to Kosovo may be a better solution than a 'full return', although donors have explicitly defined them as 'failures' (Cocozzelli, 2004).

In light of the grave consequences of the March 2004 riots, which pushed some 4500 Kosovans out of their homes, the gap between local reality and transnational conceptions of peace and multi-ethnicity is becoming ever wider. The Serb communities and individuals in the southern enclaves (whose families had resided in Kosovo for generations) targeted during the March violence were precisely those who had struggled to maintain the most neighbourly relations with their Albanian neighbours.

Unequal partnership, which accompanies the application of international concepts of peace and multi-ethnicity, also contributes to a peculiar role of Kosovan 'transnational' civil society in the local political arena. Cooperation between local NGOs and the PISG is still practically uncharted territory, even though most funding priorities for 'civil society participation' projects list the need for strong cooperation between NGOs and governmental institutions. In concrete terms lobbying and advocacy on the part of local NGOs *vis-à-vis* the PISG is considered part of the ongoing UNMIK policy of decentralization and devolution of powers. In reality, however, local NGOs express their reluctance to lobby or pressure their political elites on issues of multi-ethnic cooperation and minority return for a number of reasons:

1. Fears of appearing too political and too positive towards ethnic minorities, which may be read as jeopardizing the struggle for Kosovo independence;
2. Fears about openly siding with one or another political party;
3. Disagreement with the donor and international NGO view that local civil society must take the lead in inter-ethnic reconciliation (Llamazares & Reynolds Levy, 2003; Danida, 2004; Nietsch, 2004).

These responses may seem to be emanating from the past legacies of Kosovan parallel structures and their antipolitics or from a complete distrust of (Serbian, at the time) state authorities, as well as from local NGOs' continuous unconditional support for the political agenda of Kosovo Sovereignty (or, an unwillingness to provoke doubts about NGOs' commitment to that cause). Nevertheless, this explanation needs updating: given the severe UNMIK and EU-mandated limits on the activities and prerogatives of the PISG, especially in the sphere of minority return and integration and security issues, it seems hardly surprising that peace-building NGOs would see little reason to cooperate with or criticize the PISG. If local NGO actors were to push more openly for goals of multi-ethnic peace and integration, they would not be able to expect any reliable backing from the PISG. They might also become overly exposed and vulnerable to some 'less civil' sectors of civil society, such as the Kosovo Liberation Army veterans' associations, whose factions bear responsibility for the March 2004 violence (International Crisis Group, 2004).

There are more subtle reasons for the lack of cooperation between the NGOs and the PISG, which also demonstrate the economic and social stratification effects of the transnationalization of the local civil society sector *vis-à-vis* the rest of (non-transnationalized) Kosovan society. NGOs, on the average, employ people with higher educational and professional skills (prioritizing those with full proficiency in English) than those required by the PISG. NGO personnel also tend to receive two-to-three times higher salaries than their PISG counterparts. Consequently NGO staff may regard their colleagues in the PISG with contempt, while the latter may have reasons to doubt the NGOs' commitment to local-community or political goals. Ironically, but not surprisingly, many local NGO staff complain that they are overqualified for the tasks they are given by their Western managers. This aspect of the transnationalization of local civil society may be described as an invisible or internal 'brain drain'.

The fact that these various concerns and grievances of local NGOs and of the civil society outside them are not regularly voiced by the locals and that they pass unrecognized by international actors remains a lasting problem of foreign assistance and its skewed transnationalization of the civil society agenda. In the concrete case of international aid to Kosovo's peace building and multi-ethnicity, the multi-levelled unequal partnerships result in the lack of local *ownership of peace*. There is a relevant pre-history of the problem emerging as a global or transnational phenomenon. The outcome of a number of massive international peacekeeping operations during the 1990s was that the most powerful actors in the process—the UN, NATO, governmental agencies, the World Bank, the US government—started coalescing around a shared definition of peace and subsequent policies to design and maintain it (Llamazares & Reynolds Levy, 2003). An important part of this definition, particularly evident in the case of Kosovo, was the lack of trust in the pre-existing local political initiatives with a simultaneous belief that grassroots peace-building participation can be created from scratch in the aftermath of organized violence and state collapse. Subsequently civil society organizations, most of which were created anew, were given the disproportionately difficult task of peace building and ensuring multi-ethnic justice, as in Kosovo, while local governmental institutions were left out of the same process for years. As a result, local NGOs were forced into accepting the internationals' 'peace manuals': even when they faced no serious risk by offering their own alternative visions of peace and multi-ethnic coexistence, the possibility of not getting project funding forced them to accept a given list of priorities and problem definitions. Hence a large number of peace-building projects and a few multi-ethnic NGOs in Kosovo focus on youth initiatives or 'conversation workshops', simply because they involve hardly any political risk or controversy while fitting the bill of internationally mandated peace priorities. In the area of minority returns, as mentioned above, the lack of attention to possible alternatives to 'full return' practices and the focus on Serb IDPs in Serbia has resulted in a number of hastily implemented and failed return projects, while neglecting the needs of the minority population that remained in the southern parts of Kosovo (Cocozzelli, 2004). Many newly built residential complexes stand empty in various parts of Kosovo as a testimony to the misguided plans for minority returns.

In his 'The end of transition paradigm', Thomas Carothers criticizes the currently globally espoused and practised definition of civil society as 'social capital', where Western aid is supposed to offer assistance to post-conflict communities to build networks of mutual trust without any interference from 'top politics'. Carothers argues that designating the NGO sector in post-conflict or 'transitional' regions as simultaneously a leading 'partner' of international agendas for democratization *and* a major recipient of Western financial aid severely cripples local political capacity building (Carothers, 2002). Change must take place in the political sphere proper: more attention should be paid to placing greater responsibility upon political elites for the creation of policies that promote justice, such as ethnically non-discriminatory and affirmative action practices. Accordingly political party and governmental sphere development must take place in congruence with civil society development, and be responsible for offering a safe public arena to civil society actors. If these developments are not set in motion, calls for the foreign-assisted NGO sector to be sincere and fear no one in its commitment to justice will fall on deaf ears or create a civil society with no firm commitment to justice. The 'social capital' pragmatic paradigm of the foreign-funded civil society also tends to mask a lack of imagination or will on the part of powerful international actors, despite their rhetoric, to engage with broader populations in debating 'sensitive' political issues, such as the instability of political institutions in the aftermath of regime change, which may be, as in the cases of Bosnia and Herzegovina and Kosovo, accompanied by the entrenchment of ethno-nationalist programmes. Instead, according to a US Agency for International Development (USAID) official in Belgrade, the realm of high politics is not a major concern for civil society: "The political issues at the top are amusing entertainment, but they do not really affect people's lives" (Gordy, 2003).

There are cases where local NGOs have succeeded in simultaneously making use of local initiatives and resources and incorporating their (transnationally validated) commitment to issues of ethnic non-discrimination or minority integration, while preparing for the phasing out of major donors. Fred Cocozzelli looks at the example of Mercy Corps in Kosovo. Its activities in the area of minority return and residential reconstruction combine initiatives aimed at enhancing solidarity, some would say 'traditional', actions on the part of its constituencies (requiring local in-kind contributions) with a firm stance of advocacy and communal protection of socially marginalized groups and individuals (Cocozzelli, 2004). These local action-stimulating projects stand in contrast to the activities of the Mother Theresa Society, the former leading local NGO in Kosovo, which seems to have continued acting as a charitable, commodity-distributing organization, while only switching from local donors (before 1999) to international NGOs. Llazares and Reynolds Levy offer several positive examples of proactive peace-building projects generated by women's rights NGOs or civil society think-tanks. They have often survived their former dependence on a single donor by joining forces with other groups with similar agendas, and by diversifying their range of potential donors while sustaining their focus on particular issues. This is the case with the Kosovo Civil Society Foundation, or Kosovo Women's' Councils (Llamazares & Reynolds Levy, 2003).

In the concrete political context of Kosovo, potential risks contingent upon the instrumentalization of civil society in pursuing tough political goals, as well as delayed corresponding action in the sphere of political institution building, have been aggravated by the inability of international actors to determine the final status of Kosovo. The top-down realization of particular definitions of peace here implies the UNMIK-mandated 'Standards [of European governance] before Status' course of action, which, while imagined as a mechanism of gradual state-building in Kosovo, is most often used as a tool for suppressing public debate on 'sensitive' political issues. Since the issues of multi-ethnicity and inter-ethnic cooperation are most susceptible to political repercussions, their transnationalization is, thus, accompanied in practice by the discouraging of local civil society groups to engage in any consideration of their serious implementation.

The most encouraging result of the enormous culpability that was laid on the shoulders of UNMIK and KFOR after the March 2004 violence was the pressure to reformulate the implications of the 'Standards before Status' policy. As the chronic lack of motivation on the part of local NGOs to engage in serious cooperation with the PISG demonstrates, local political institutions and Kosovo Albanian parties were granted little power and, subsequently, little responsibility to work on some of the crucial Standards areas pertaining to peace building, such as freedom of movement or sustainable returns. On the other hand, Serbs living in the north of Kosovo under the patronage of Serbia and their parallel institutions saw little benefit in participating in the fulfilment of the Standards. It is still unclear whether or not powerful international actors have recognized that the 'Standards before Status' do little to delegitimize the confrontational and ethno-centred political model of action in Kosovo. However, at least at the level of NGO-led debates, there is some growing understanding, shared by both parts of Kosovo, that the final status agreement must incorporate and reflect the following real pressures:

- the inevitability and necessity of open borders between Kosovo and Serbia, given the economic and ethnic ties and mix;
- the dependence of both Kosovo and Serbia on the accession procedures of the European Union (EU).

One may hope that Kosovan NGOs will turn these newly gained certainties about where Kosovo stands into new definitions of peace building, which depend more on the feedback from their beneficiaries than on donors, and more on shared responsibilities with local authorities than on covert party allegiances.

Learning from Everyday Life and Economic Travails

As Thomas Carothers points pout, international aid-providing agencies must become involved in building political capacity in post-conflict or 'transitional' regions, which should replace or complement their insistence on 'social capital' as a product of non-politicized civil society (Carothers, 2002). Equally important, in the case of Kosovo, is the process of learning about peace and inter-ethnic coexistence from the realm of everyday life or non-institutionalized civil society.

In the city of Prizren, multi-ethnicity or a local version of multiculturalism, in the form of multilingual practices and non-segregated economic life, has survived the apartheid of the1990s and the violence of 1998–99. In the towns of Gjilan/Gnjilane and Lipjan/ Lipljan a similar type of multiculturalism came about as the result of the combination of liberal local government, several successful multi-ethnic endeavours (schools and kindergartens, and a US KFOR-supported business association), and a relatively low level of war destruction. In the March 2004 riots these success stories and areas came under attack, which many interpreted as simply a manifestation of the fragility of local civil society. One should also observe that the severity of the violence in these areas might have been a sign of the deep disturbance that a bottom-up improvement in inte-rethnic relations and reintegration activities caused for the exclusionary agendas of the uncivil and armed segments of local civil society.

One finds the most striking examples of non-hostile inter-ethnic relations in Kosovo in its southeastern region of Anamorava, where 30% of the population is non-Albanian, and where little donor money has so far been spent, but where the dairy plant in the village of Kusce, belonging to an Albanian owner, has a multi-ethnic workforce and regularly attracts Serb farmers. The Borovci Brothers brick factory in the vicinity of Gjilan, a rare successful privatization story, also attracts a multi-ethnic labour force. The factory was bought from the Kosovo Trust Agency that carries the UN mandate for selling former state enterprises. The new owners had to fulfil the requirements of multi-ethnic staff composition. One explanation for not there not being more such success stories is that the 'Standards before Status' policies prevent the sale of a number of large industrial complexes whose facilities lie in both parts of Kosovo (Berisha *et al.*, 2004). Conversations with the unemployed former workers of the Trepča/Trepça mining complex, which used to employ tens of thousands of miners and workers across Kosovo until the late 1980s, and was closed down in 1999 because of environmental hazard issues, offer an insight into the primary grievances of ordinary people being only indirectly affected by ethno-nationalist programmes.

What worries local business owners in eastern Kosovo, especially those in farming and dairy production, is less the state of ethnic segregation or sovereignty than the implications of the new relaxed customs regime with the European Union. The reality of the EU's lauded 'open doors' economic policy is that it has made it virtually impossible for local producers to compete with Western agricultural imports, while facing numerous sanitary and quality obstacles when trying to export to the EU (Gjurgjeala, 2005). The grim reality of local farmers lies between the EU rhetoric of open markets and its inability to offer subsidies to Balkan farmers similar to those enjoyed by their counterparts in the 'core' EU. It also rests with the weakness of governments, such as those in Serbia, UNMIK-Kosovo, Bosnia and Herzegovina, or Albania, that cannot undertake any serious restructuring of agriculture on their own.

Echoing examples from the arena of everyday life and economic practices, in particular those from the three municipalities of the Anamorava region, some local critics of the 'Standard before Status' policies in Kosovo emphasize that 'multi-ethnicity' and 'multi-culturalism' are irritating terms for locals, as they seem to imply that there was no multi-ethnic Kosovo before 1999, and that it can exist only as a standard to be tried and achieved before the decision on the final status of Kosovo. Some critics suggest that the fact that 'multi-ethnicity' has become part of the Standards before Status (and simultaneously a lasting fad for the NGO world) has also turned even the most banal instances of inter-ethnic communication into a hostage of high politics in Kosovo.[4] A startling example of such hijacking of multi-ethnicity issues is the use of the Serb (or Croat, or Bosnian) language in everyday life in the two largest cities of Priština/Prishtina or Mitrovica. While it may be spoken between non-Albanian speakers and Albanians in private settings, it is considered taboo in public spaces. In this way local practices of inter-ethnic relations have been gradually pushed out of everyday life. With respect to particular experiences of the most vulnerable groups, i.e. local Roma, their situation in the aftermath of the 1999 intervention and the change in Kosovo's status has been reduced to that of a non-state-constituent ethnicity (the lowest-class minority), which has resulted in their lasting neglect at the hands and in the minds of international donors and, consequently, of the transnationalized local aid industry. Inter-ethnic relations are thus continuously reconstituted as a fundamental part of the zero-sum game of ethno-centric sovereignty.

With regard to the use of minority and majority languages in everyday life, it is relevant to place them in the context of other informal patterns of inter-ethnic relations in Kosovo. Informal intel-ethnic and cross-border ties work clandestinely but exceptionally well between powerful but illegitimate figures, such as smugglers of goods and people, which even improved in their density and cooperativeness during the war years, following the allure of profits that could be extracted through high-risk trans-border trade at the time, as Aida Hozic documents in her work on Balkan cigarette smuggling (Hozic, 2004), as well as in her article in this issue of Ethnopolitics. Somewhat less clandestine but also less shielded is the communication among people in the few legitimate economic enterprises which employ multiethnic labor force, whom I described in the beginning of this section. The least protected and most unpublicized are private inter-ethnic contacts between (former) neighbors and friends, especially in cases where they had protected each other against acts of ethnic cleansing (as in the cases of Serbs sheltering Albanians during the 1999 NATO bombing campaign and the Serbian Army-led expulsion of Albanian civillllians).

Western donors-sponsored local NGOs organized meetings between people of different ethnicities, which mainly fall in the category of "reconciliation meetings", while receiving accolades for proving that Albanians and Serbs can talk to each other on conference panels, often bring together local Albanians and Serbs who do not live in Kosovo. Numerous projects targeting youth bring to Kosovo students from Belgrade or Macedonia, where all enjoy good time and vow to spread the spirit of tolerance in their home locales. These instances of misguided foreign intervention (alas, inadvertently) further the point that there is nothing hisorically "natural" or continuous about the negative attitudes that Albanians have toward Serbs and the other way around. There is a remaining lesson unlearnt in these "tolerance-teaching" projects that cultural and ethnic differences are not a problem per se, but that they are fed by the agendas of mutually irreconcilable projects of ethnicity-centered sovereignty which Western donors do not object to. Hence, if you live in Kosovo, public succumbing to top-down pressures not to communicate with ethnic "others" (minorities of today) may, paradoxically, coexist with privately held tolerant or even positive attitudes and memories of inter-ethnic coexistence.

It is also tempting to examine and compare trans-border exchange and consumption in the realm of popular culture, and popular music consumption in particular, as part of civil society exercise in inter-ethnic relations, between Kosovo and other regions of the former Yugoslavia that were at war with each other during the 1990s.[5] Just as Catherine Baker outlines in this volume, during the war in Croatia in 1991–1993, which coincided with its struggle for state independence, pop and rock musicians were at the cultural forefront of the efforts to vilify and "otherzie" the Serb enemy, as an alien presence both within and outside Croatia: writing and singing patriotic songs, some volunteering for the army. Nevertheless, following the war, pop and rock music industry has quickly acquired a relatively relaxed and oblivious stance toward its war-time nationalist endeavors, abandoning their vows to sever all ties-with the enemy ethnics.

The above transformation of popular culture protagonists should only seem as a paradox to those observers who were prone to believe that nationalist mobilization in the former Yugoslavia was a force from below, a bursting of the supposedly most widely shared desires for ethically homogenous states. Ten years later, when public opinion polls show that (former) nationalist politicians and other members of political and cultural elites display a more positive and relaxed attitude toward former "enemy ethnics" than ordinary people, these observers could seem to be right (Opacic & Vujadinovic, 2005). But one should not forgot to compare these polls to a number of other surveys conducted in Yugoslavia since the late 1980s until the outbreak of violence, which demonstrate that the stitting of ethnonationalist fears (first) and hostilities (next) went from top of bottom, involving, first and foremost, (ex-) Communist Party *nomenklatura*, and, second, the most influential Communist-era cultural and academic institutions, -while it took hold among ordinary people only after the erutpion of violence, such as the building of road blocks by Croatian Serbs in the Krajina region in the summer of 1990 (Hodson, Massey, & Sekulic 1993; Lazic, 1993, Devic, 1998).

We may then offer a diagnosis of the present distribution of cooperative and hostile inter-ethnic attitudes among the different social strata that differs from the one that attributes the outbreak of ethnoationalist wars to the long-seated inter-ethnic animosities. It may be that following the cessation of violence and the establishment of new states on the ashes of Yugoslavia, the elite strata that had managed to preserve or augment their economic and symbolic capital during or even because of the war and state-building years would be the fist one to strive to benefit from reaching out to the former enemies, now re-emerging as neighbors. In the case of political elites, their new good relations with former enemy states (Serbia, Croatia, Bosnia-Herzegovina) also bring possibilities of advances in the realm of the new European Union-oriented (and dependent on it) hierarchies and organizations (various commissions in charge of the EU-accession proces).

In the sphere of popular music, its makers have benefited from and continued in the footsteps of the longtime Yugoslav pop and rock music market, and related networks of cooperation. Given the enormous popularity of major Croatian, Serbian and Bosnian pop, rock and turbo folk stars across the Dayton Triangle state borders, and the related strengthening of collaboration between the most successful song composers, lyric writers, and various managers who guarantee that that popularity continues to bring huge revenues in legitimate and controlled fashion, rather than falling in the hands of pirate music traders (as was the case during the war), it can be suggested that ordinary people in the region cannot follow their elites in displaying cooperative inter-ethnic attitudes simply because they lack adequate resources to do so. Among these resources the most important one is access to spatial mobility, which includes free movement across borders. Today, it requires much greater economic costs that it was the case before the war. The movement is also hampered by political and administrative barriers, such as visa regimes (visas between Croatia and Serbia were abolished only two and half years ago), and the lack of interest among major local news media in disseminating information about the neighboring parts of former Yugoslav popular culture celebrities and consumption excess of all nouveau riches in the region). It comes as no surprise, then, that enormous trans-border consumption of the same ex-pan-Yugoslav popular music product becomes the sole manifestation and a "sublimated" proxy of cultural ties between the ordinary people in the region. To what extent this sublimation can be repeated in Kosovo, where forced inter-ethnic segregation has lasted for nearly 20 years (since the advent to power of Slobodan Milosevic) and were the struggle for ethno-centered state sovereignty is far from being over, remains to be seen. In the meantime, one must deplore the poor interest and investment of foreign donors in the realm of popular culture market and traditions of its consumption in the region.

Conclusion: Some Caveats of Exporting Multiculturalism to Post-socialist States

As a proposal for reconsideration of the links between ethnicity or ethno-nationality and the civil society agenda in Kosovo, I will now consider the applicability of the concepts and norms of liberal ethno-multiculturalism in post-socialist multi-ethnic spaces, such as former Yugoslavia or states formerly belonging to the Soviet Union. Just as the previously mentioned 'coalescing definition' of peace building of the international peace brokers in Kosovo stifles local meanings of peace that may be informed by everyday life experiences and grievances, so the export of liberal multiculturalism to post-violence zones often neglects both the local realities that preceded the violence and alternative practices of inter-ethnic relations that may not seek to institutionalize the majority–minority divide (for typical a–sociological advices on how to define–cum–manage majority–minority relations in the post–socialist region see, for example, Kymlicka, 2001a; 2001b). It is not difficult to see that, in both ethno-nationally politicized settings in

Kosovo and among international actors promoting liberal multiculturalism, inter-ethnic relations on the ground are defined as a 'problem to be treated'. This formulation of *the* problem tends to obscure rather dramatic differences between the practice of inter-ethnic relations on the ground in Kosovo, and 'multi-ethnicity' as a problematic internationally mandated standard to be met. The following question, then, may be put. Can the theory and policies of liberal ethno-multiculturalism offer a model for institutionalizing justice in the post-socialist East–Central Europe when the transition to democracy has been preconditioned by conflicts organized along ethnic lines, which achieved an unprecedented ethnic un-mixing and homogenization, creating 'majorities' and 'minorities' in the region where they did not exist before.

No region, and southeastern Europe is no exception, is a blank slate of neatly separated culturally homogeneous groups. The most discomforting question, perhaps, for advocates of exporting liberal ethno-multiculturalism to Eastern Europe is: how do groups become homogeneous and separated? How do their cultural institutions acquire a political character and, thus, endow culture with a conflict potential? When one faces the course and consequences of the violence of the past decade in the former Yugoslav region, harrowing answers to these questions overshadow and tarnish any enthusiasm for an ideal space of groups having an equal and divided 'ethno-cultural ownership' of the state:

> The various efforts to forcibly change the distribution of ethnic populations in the region (whether we label these efforts as 'ethnic cleansing,' 'genocide,' or some other term) have been, for the most part, successful. More so than before, the region is characterized by a series of relatively homogeneous enclaves to which refugees are largely unwilling to return—the exceptions are places that were not directly affected by violence. Although areas that are under international governance are seeing the imposition of a kind of structured multiculturalism (imposed with some limited success in the Federation entity of Bosnia-Herzegovina, and with no discernible success in Kosovo), in other areas the domination of majorities has become established in a way that is only weakly contested. (Gordy, 2002)

The question that ought to be asked is: in what ways can we be assured that post-communist nationalisms will not stray into illiberal forms? Should we not first suppose that the causes of inter-ethnic violence and subsequent ethnic un-mixing of the region are possibly *not* rooted in the communist-era suppression of ethnic organizing and the institutionalization of ethnicity? As Katherine Verdery (1998) and Roger Brubaker (1996) show, ethnic violence and state re-mappings in the aftermath of 1989 have been facilitated by the pre-existing long-time confederal organization of multi-ethnic socialist states into 'national republics' led by local ethnic cadres. Communist parties in Yugoslavia and the Soviet Union introduced this organization of political space several decades before the breakdown of communism—as a proxy for and solution to the deficits of proclaimed democratization and the alleged pinnacle of the will for freedom of their people that would later be turned into the will of peoples![6] In other words, the post-1989 redrawing of state maps was charted by the socialist-era cultivation of 'ethnic cadres', who then reinvented themselves as post-communist ethno-political 'entrepreneurs' (to use Katherine Verdery's and Ronnie Lipschutz's (1998) term).

The success of these ethnic entrepreneurs was, ironically, additionally facilitated by international pressure for democratization. In the absence of any developed democratic constituency and a plural political arena, claims for the institutionalization of ethno-nationality and the subsequent division of citizens into majorities and minorities have become the main instruments of maximizing votes. In the Yugoslav context:

> In a society that had been characterized by a complex long-time social and economic crisis, such as the one that pervaded the Yugoslav society during the 1980s, ethnicity became a vehicle of the consolidation of patronage networks of political control during the transition from the Communist to pluralist political framework. (Oberschall, 2000)

Numerous accounts of the violent and organized character of the protracted breakdown of the Yugoslav state place serious doubt on the applicability of the thesis that ethnic autonomies and ethnic politics are the best remedies for the democratic deficit in post-socialist and post-violence multi-ethnic states. Even if we accept the package of 'ethno cultural justice' as a useful impetus for protecting minority languages and cultural institutions, we ought to be reminded that in the areas and periods where individual rights and economic existence are precarious, insistence on collective rights tied to ascribed ethnic markers of citizenship may act as further hindrance of democratic participation. The politics of ethnicity in the post-Yugoslav space, such as in Serbia, Kosovo, Bosnia and Herzegovina, or in the former republics of the Soviet Union, shows that the interest of local elites in the tenets of liberal multiculturalism–nationalism may be motivated less by their democratization agendas than by their need to bypass the imperatives of broader political participation of their constituencies. These imperatives are, instead, redefined in terms of a balance between 'state-constitutive' ethnic majorities versus ethnic minorities.

There are, then, two main problems with liberal multiculturalism that bear relevance to both multi-ethnic post-socialist 'transitional' states and Western industrialized societies. One is the identification of ethnic identity with all culture, or prioritization of ethnicity above all cultural traits, and the other is the assumption that such ethnicized culture is the primary basis for the political organization of ethnic minorities in democratic societies (Vermeulen & Slijper, 2002). In the context of the post-socialist states of East–Central and southeastern Europe these erroneous premises achieve a state of dangerous affinity with the interests of nationalist elites who, during the past decade, have striven to redraw state boundaries and justified their agendas with claims of defending 'their own' communities. In the realm of culture in post-socialist societies, identification of one ethnicity with all cultural life and with the paramount political interest serves to deny both the reality and possibility of inter-ethnic identities, as well as broader venues for alternative or oppositional political mobilization.

For local post-socialist elites, that is, ethnic entrepreneurs, liberal multiculturalism and liberal nationalism simultaneously affirm their own (violently) homogenized imaginings of political space and satisfy prescriptions for democratization coming from the West. They help deny or neglect the evidence that before the outbreaks of violence there existed some long-standing forms of multiculture, which could be defined as unstructured multiculturalism, rooted in everyday life and indicating the existence of alternatives to liberal multiculturalism (Gagnon, 2001; Gordy, 2002).

It may not sound at the moment like a realist politician's preferred option, but it is nevertheless compelling to imagine and propose that the inhabitants of post-socialist multi-ethnic states could wrestle out, and be assisted in building, a kind of citizen membership and public space that draws upon the realities of their own recent past.[7] The restoration of multiculturality in the Kosovan political space would necessarily involve an articulation of alternatives to the imagining of individual persons as primarily ethno-nationals. Until then there is another reminder of the misguided and unjust social and economic projects in the region pertaining to multi-ethnic coexistence: the trans-ethnic and truly multinational character of illegal trade networks in the post-socialist Balkans, which simultaneously cross borders while thriving on their post-cold war multiplicity, offer their own twisted image of citizens liberated from ethno-national programmes, as masterfully illustrated and explained in their relation to global economy by Aida Hozic in this volume. My analysis of the misconceptions about local civil society, which inform the agenda of western aid to peace and multiculturalism in Kosovo illustrate and support Hozic's theses on misrepresentations of the Social role and the stigmatization of Balkan illicit trade networks, which simultaneously attempt to make inter-state borders porous, while thriving on their post-Cold War multiplicity. The flourishing (but also precarious) illicit trade, (now mostly) legal cross-border popular music market, as well as the secret, unpublicized and unpopular private inter-ethnic ties within and across Yugoslavia's successor states, are simultaneously opposing, while being dependant on (or suffering from) the newly erected nation state boundaries and European Union re-bordering practices. Hozic's powerful "global merchants" trade protectionism and new obstacles to migration (which is defined as "right to free movement"-for Western citizens only), which marginalize both Balkan small merchants and ordinary people, serve to sim-ultaneously respond to and mock, as one of the weapons of the weak, the global asymme-trical access to transnational resources and identities, embedded, as Hozic demonstrates, in the contradiction between state sovereignty and meta-national flows of capital and culture. This study sought to demonstrate how the local civil society, whose potentials and histori-cal (dis)continuities have been largely unrecognized and even weakened by Western aid agencies, at least, serves to question and sabotage the alleged immutability and autarky of local ethnonational identities.

Notes

1. Local government institutions have been in place since 2002 as part of the devolution of power from the UN to local authorities. Foreign policy, minority return, military sector and security issues are still prerogatives of the UN, NATO and the EU organizations.
2. This typology of societal participation in projects of Western civil society assistance was developed by Sarah C. White (1996).
3. For these estimates, see the European Stability Initiative (2004) report.
4. I draw here on my interviews with and personal communication from Leon Malazogu, research director of the Kosovan Institute for Policy Research and Development (KIPRED); Fadil Maloku, executive director of the Institute for Democracy and Ethnic Relations of Kosovo; and Enver Hasani, a professor of international law and international relations at Priština University.
5. Even though at the first sight it may seen that the comparison may be flawed since popular music is written and sung in the same language across the Dayton Triangle, we should be reminded that during the war and state-consolidating years in Serbia, Croatia and Bosnia-Herzegovina, the language that was previously considered the same and shared under the name of Serbo-Croat, had become divided into three languages (now, with the independence of montenegro, it will be four) each claiming and forging Substantial differences from its former parts (which were previously termed as dialectical and regional varieties).
6. Susan L. Wodward (1995) details the process of decentralization or devolution of political rule from federal to republican and municipal levels in the socialist Yugoslavia. She demonstrates how in a

one-party regime and in the absence of political pluralism, where each federal republic had one (or three, in the case of Bosnia-Herzegovina) 'titular' ethno-nationalities, decentralization led to the emergence of economic and political autarky and latent rivalry between the nationalist republican leaderships.

7. Chip Gagnon (2001) explains how Western aid efforts have so far impeded instead of assisted the rebuilding of multicultural spaces of everyday life in southeastern Europe. Gagnon argues that Western imaginings of a liberal polity have rested upon the often violent practice of ethnic homogenization which accompanied Western state-building projects.

References

Brubaker, R. (1996) *Nationalism Reframed: Nationhood and the National Question in the New Europe* (Cambridge: Cambridge University Press).

Carothers, T. (2002) The end of the transition paradigm, *Journal of Democracy*, 13(1), pp. 5–21.

Cocozzelli, F. (2004) The political situation in Kosovo in 2004 and the challenges it presents, final paper for the IUCSHA Fellowship, available online at: http://web.gc.cuny.edu/RalphBuncheInstitute/IUCSHA/fellows/Cocozzelli-final%20paper.pdf.

Danida (Danish Ministry of Foreign Affairs) (2004) *Evaluation: Humanitarian and Rehabilitation Assistance to Kosovo, 1999–2003*, available online at: http://www.um.dk/Publikationer/Danida/English/Evaluations/Kosovo2005/Kosovo.pdf.

Devic, A. (1998) Ethnonationalism, Politics, and the Intellectuals: The case of Yugoslavia, International Journal of Politics, culture and society, 11(3).

European Stability Initiative (2004) *The Lausanne Principle: Multiethnicity, Territory and the Future of Kosovo's Serbs*, report available online at: http://www.esiweb.org/pdf/esi_document_id_53.pdf.

Gagnon, V. P. (2001) Serbs as victims and perpetrators of violence, paper presented at the conference on Comparative Minority Issues, Vienna, 11–14 April 2001.

Gjurgjeala, J. (2005) EU offers Balkan farmers a bleak harvest, *Institute for War and Peace Reporting Balkan Crisis Report (IWPR)*, 535, 10 January. http://ww.iwpr.net/?p=bcr&s=f&o=155710&apc_state=henibcr2005

Gordy, E. (2002) Obstacles to multiculturality in the contemporary Balkans, paper presented at the annual conference of the Association for the Study of Nationalities, Centro per l'Europa centro-orientale e balcanica, Forli, June.

Gordy, E. (2003) CRDA and civil society in Serbia, *Muabet Project Report*, Watson Institute for International Studies, available online at: http://www.watsoninstitute.org/muabet/new_site/reports.cfm.

Hodson, R. Massey, G. & Sekulic, D. (1993) National Tolerance in the Former Yugoslavia, Global Forum Series occasional papers (Durham, N.C: Center for International Studies, Duke University), 93-01.5.

Hozic, A. (2004) Between the Cracks: Balkan Cigarette Smuggling, *Problems of Post-Communism* 51 May–June (3), pp. 35–44.

International Crisis Group (2004) Collapse in Kosovo, *Europe Report 155*, 22 April, available online at: http://www.crisisweb.org/home/index.cfm.

Konrad, G. (1984) *Antipolitics* (New York: Holt).

Kymlicka, W. (2001a) Western political theory and ethnic relations in Eastern Europe, in: W. Kymlicka & M. Opalski (Eds), *Can Liberal Pluralism be Exported? Western Political Theory and Ethnic Relations in Eastern Europe*, pp. 13–105 (New York: Oxford University Press).

Kymlicka, W. (2001b) Reply and conclusion, in: W. Kymlicka & M. Opalski (Eds), *Can Liberal Pluralism be Exported? Western Political Theory and Ethnic Relations in Eastern Europe*, pp. 345–413 (New York: Oxford University Press).

Lazic, M. (1993) The level of National Absorption, in K. Prpic, B. Despot, & N. Dugandzija (Eds), *The Myth of "Ethnic conflicit": Politics, Economics, and "Cultural" Violence* (Berkeley: University of California Press).

Lipschutz, R. D. (1998) Seeking a state of one's own: an analytical framework for assessing ethnic and sectarian conflicts, in: B. Crawford & R. D. Lipschutz (Eds), *The Myth of 'Ethnic Conflict': Politics, Economics, and 'Cultural' Violence* (Berkeley, CA: University of California Press).

Maliqi, Sh. (1996) The Albanian movement in Kosova, in D. A. Dyker & I. Vejvoda (Eds), *Yugoslavia and After*, pp. 138–154 (New York: Longman).

Llamazares, M. & Reynolds Levy, L. (2003) NGOs and peacebuilding in Kosovo, *Working Paper No. 13*, Centre for Conflict Resolution, Bradford, available online at: http://www.centreforconflictresolution.org.uk.

Berisha, L., Bekteshi, D. & Antic, S. (2004) Ethnic divide bridged in south-east Kosovo, *Institute for War and Peace Reporting (IWPR)*, 520, 9 October 2004.

Nietsch, J. (2004) Civil society in Kosovo: the interaction between local NGOs and the Provisional Institutions of Self-Government, working paper of the Austrian Institute for International Affairs/Österreichisches Institut für Internationale politik (www.oiip.at).

Oberschall, A. (2000) The manipulation of ethnicity: from ethnic cooperation to violence and war in Yugoslavia, *Ethnic and Racial Studies*, 23(6), pp. 982–1002.

Opacic, G. & Vujadinovic, B. (2005) Etnicke distance i ethnicki stereotipi kao faktor odluke o povratku, in Goran Opacic & Branko Vujadinovic (Eds), *Zivot u posleratnim Zajednicama* (Belgrade: IAN) available online at http://www.ian.org.yu/publikacije

Tarrow, S. (1998) *Power in Movement: Social Movements and Contentious Politics* (Cambridge: Cambridge University Press).

Verdery, K. (1998) Transnationalism, nationalism, citizenship, and property, *American Ethnologist*, 25(2), pp. 291–306.

Vermeulen, H. & Slijper, B. (2002) Multiculturalism and culturalism. A social scientific critique of the political philosophy of multiculturalism: nationalism, regional multiculturalism and democracy, *ZEI European Studies and South Eastern Europe Papers*, SEE 2, available online at: http://www.zei.de/download/zei_soe/see_02_2002.pdf.

White, S. C. (1996) Depoliticising development: the uses and abuses of participation, *Development in Practice*, 6(1), pp. 6–15.

Woodward, S. L. (1995) *Balkan Tragedy: Chaos and Dissolution after the Cold War* (Washington, DC: Brookings Institution).

The Politics of Performance: Transnationalism and its Limits in Former Yugoslav Popular Music, 1999–2004

CATHERINE BAKER

Former Yugoslavia and Transnational Cultural Spaces

With the disintegration of Yugoslavia, musical activities, which had previously taken place within one domestic market, were necessarily re-contextualized as transnational flows of information, culture and capital. In parallel with the political changes in Croatia and Serbia following the death of the Croatian president Franjo Tudjman in 1999 and the fall of the Serbian president Slobodan Milošević in 2000, the extension of cultural contacts enabled now-transnational musical relations between the two successor states to be re-established as legitimate recording, distribution and performance activities rather than the 'underground' practices they had largely been throughout the 1990s. This paper focuses on the re-establishment period between 2000 and 2004, when decisions on whether or not to perform 'across the border' were invested with political significance by musicians and the media. At stake, from a Croatian viewpoint, was whether the national cultural space should continue to be defined by the enclosed, nationalizing criteria of the 1990s, and to what extent it should accommodate newly transnational cultural products, which connoted the Yugoslav era, or a present-day ethnic Other.

The concept of a transnational community employed here follows Ulf Hannerz in encompassing a "fairly continuous negotiation of meanings, values, and symbolic forms...involving the cultures of the old place and the new place" (Hannerz, 1996, pp. 99–100). Analysing migration alone also acknowledges other ways in which transnational flows of people, capital or cultural products may influence individual identities (Jackson *et al.*, 2004, p. 2). This broader approach may be applied to former Yugoslavia, to take in not only those who crossed state borders during the 1990s' wartime upheaval, but also many others who were still left with multiple, and sometimes irreconcilable, identities, since Yugoslavia's disintegration and the re-interpretation of formerly domestic phenomena engendered many ambiguities and tensions also experienced by transnational migrants.

Moreover, post-Yugoslav cultural spaces have also witnessed the "transnational syncretism" described by Thomas Faist as the "diffusion of culture and [the] emergence of new types—mixed identities" (Faist, 2000, p. 201). Allowance must be made here for those whose displacement was a matter of "symbolic and imaginary" geography rather than the "material" kind (Jackson *et al.*, 2004, p. 3). Alongside the familiar concept of spatial transnationalism, indeed, there may also exist a *temporal* form, shaped by pronounced discontinuity between the new state narratives and some individuals' personal experience. Such individuals, just like those who are more conventionally the stock-in-trade of transnational studies, were obliged to negotiate their conflicting identities and—albeit temporally rather than spatially—placed in the same circumstances of existing simultaneously in more than one social field.

One typology of approaches to transnationalism includes its function as a means of "cultural reproduction" (Vertovec, 1999, p. 451)—a suitable departure-point from which to analyse popular music's position in the (spatial and temporal) transnationalism of former Yugoslavia. For other theorists, too, "the collective enjoyment of cultural events and goods" constitutes a definite aspect of transnationalism (Portes *et al.*, 1999, p. 221). Popular music is a significant form in this respect: not only do individual consumers select "meanings, pleasures and social identities" by choosing one musical product over another (Fiske, 1987, p. 311), but they also express their identities socially by making value judgements about music (Russell, 1997, p. 151), using particular allusions as "boundary-markers" to project definitions of one's own group and of others' (Cohen, 1985, p. 12). Musical figures who are now considered to be transnational play a particularly strong part in this symbolism. Furthermore, the representations in the texts of "a mass-mediated image culture" may be highly revealing of sociopolitical ideology (Kellner, 1995, p. 60); and the controversies surrounding transnational musical activity—particularly in Croatia—have indeed offered insights into the formation of the national ethnopolitical discourse, and of similar discourses of identity.

The full matrix of former Yugoslav transnational musical flows is at least six-sided, but this paper focuses on the relationship between Croatian and Serbian musical products. The paper first reviews Croatian musical activity in Serbia and Montenegro, and Serbian musical activity in Croatia, before concentrating on Croatia to examine how certain musicians with (licit or illicit) transnational audiences have become symbolic resources for constructing a number of possible Croatian identities. Finally, it discusses the position of newly composed folk music as itself a transnational cultural form.

Croatian Musical Activity in Serbia–Montenegro and Slovenia

Croatian artists' decisions to perform in Serbia and Montenegro have provoked polemics; indeed, even just after Franjo Tudjman's death in December 1999, too many performances 'across the border' might still have risked a mainstream pop-schlager (*zabavna*) artist's career.[1] In late 1999 several *zabavna* singers and groups were approached by concert organizers from Serbia and Montenegro, but criticism from the Croatian media centred on Doris Dragović when she was alleged to have agreed to perform in a Montenegrin resort for New Year 2000 alongside Hari Varešanović, Haris Džinović and Maja Nikolić (Lacko, 1999).[2] While offering a lucrative commercial opportunity, the Montenegrin appearance provoked the influential president of the Croatian Musicians' Union (HGU), Paolo Sfeci, to remark that Dragović should "think about whether and how much her decision will have an effect on her career and image in Croatia" (Djilas, 1999).[3] It inflicted long-term damage to Dragović's following among Hajduk Split's Torcida fan-club (Gall, 2001a). Earlier in the decade, singing the 1992 patriotic song '*Dajem ti srce*' ('I give you my heart'), Dragović had assimilated into her performance persona the maternal gender role inherent in Tudjman's conception of the nation (Senjković, 2002, p. 149), where a woman's primary duty was to bear children for the national collective and ensure the historical continuity of the Croat people. These associations may partly account for Dragović's position at the centre of the scandal.

At the height of this case Alka Vuica (another invited performer) wrote an article for the Croatian weekly *Nacional* describing it as "the ultimate hypocrisy" to attack singers while Croatian entrepreneurs had re-established commercial (and sporting) relations with Serbia in all other respects (Djilas, 1999). Vuica, too, has been affected by her early willingness to perform in Serbia and Montenegro, and has arguably been more popular there than in her home country. This may be explained by her affection for overtly 'Balkan' musical elements and her frequent use of Serbian, Macedonian, Greek, and Turkish motifs and cover versions, aligning her with the "popular Balkan (counter) culture" described by Alexander Kiossev, which celebrates such elements as positive signs of identification (Kiossev, 2002, pp. 184–5).[4] This, and her level of cultural–political engagement (which is unusual on the Croatian popular music scene), marks her as distinct in a cultural environment suffused with ambivalence towards the concept of the Balkans.[5]

Yet little or no reaction was provoked by the Belgrade concerts a year later given by Darko Rundek and the punk band KUD Idijoti (Grujičić, 2000). However, these artists belong to the rock discourse, where performers and consumers may define their product against both mass-market showbusiness and nationalistic chauvinism,[6] while *zabavna* singers, far more dependent on mass-media channels, are far more vulnerable to their disapproval. Vuica's treatment of popular music as another aspect of commercial relations overlooks its cherished symbolic value as the cultural space of a national community, emphasized in the attempts made to establish certain genres as symbols of Croat, Serb or Muslim identity (Laušević, 2000, pp. 293–4). Only by 2001–02 had Serbia and Montenegro become viewed as acceptable territory on which Croatian singers might perform, with the band Magazin undertaking a late 2001 Serbian tour and the singer Severina supporting a Djordje Balašević concert in Novi Sad (Goreta, 2002).

The significance of performances in Serbia continued to be understood in Croatia on a deeper level than the purely commercial, and a small number of artists, including Giuliano (a member of the far-right Croatian Party of Right (HSP)) and Mate Mišo Kovač (whose son died early in the war in Croatia), have refused outright to perform there (Marinović, 2001; Blažević, 2004).[7] Nonetheless, Croatian performers continue to make their Serbian debuts, while a handful of singers, including Maja Šuput and Sandi Cenov, regularly participate at festivals in Budva and Herceg Novi which assemble singers from throughout ex-Yugoslavia. In March 2003 Croatian bands and singers such as Magazin, Severina, Boris Novković, Crvena jabuka and Karma received awards at a Belgrade ceremony organized by Serbia's TV Pink, the first such event to assemble musicians from all the ex-Yugoslav states (Strukar, 2003b). The process has been assisted by the regularization of discographic activity: rather than being re-sold in pirate editions as in the 1990s, Croatian CDs and cassettes are now produced under licence by Serbian record companies, which frequently commit artists to promotional appearances. However, the amount of coverage this receives from the Croatian media is not commensurate with the performers' Serbian popularity. Recording and performance activity in Serbia itself no longer brings the opprobrium of the immediate post-Tudjman era, but still represents a parallel career for Croatian artists, with success in Serbia rarely presented as a matter of course in the public personae they offer to the domestic media.

The transnational reach of TV Pink, based in Serbia (where the channel has been strongly associated since the Milošević era with showbusiness–folk music, but also with the introduction of 1990s music-video production values into Serbian music promotion (Kronja, 2001, pp. 42–45)) but available on satellite throughout the ex-Yugoslav region, is one example of the modern entertainment media's ability to frustrate the establishment of separate national cultural spaces.[8] Another is the emergence of internet sites providing legal or illegal access to pre-1991 and contemporary music, alongside transnationally available web pages which transmit publicity and gossip to an audience beyond national borders. This transnational consumption is restricted to users of the necessary technology. Yet, as opportunities for internet access grow, they provide an increasingly significant channel for individuals to acquire transnational frames of reference towards popular culture, and compensate for the continued marginalization of other successor states' music in the mass-circulation media. The establishment of an MTV franchise for former Yugoslavia—branded as MTV Adria and initially available only in Slovenia, Croatia, and Bosnia-Herzegovina (Rašević, 2005)—represents a further phase of this development: the commercialization of an aspirational ideal of musical transnationalism, as if only so-called 'urban culture' (as opposed to 'turbofolk') could be described as transnational.

Like Serbia, Slovenia provides Croatian musicians with another potentially lucrative site of activity and media promotion, and in the 1990s represented the principal foreign market for the Croatian record industry. However, within the Slovenian context, Croatian artists belong to the analytically fascinating framework of *bivša domača* (former domestic) music: Croatian, Serbian, Montenegrin, Bosnian and Macedonian artists are aggregated into a conceptual whole which reinforces Slovenes' perception of distinctiveness from the other ex-Yugoslav peoples (Velikonja, 2002, p. 189), but also their consciousness of having *in the past* belonged to the Yugoslav community.[9] Regardless of the extent to which Croatian identity is also defined against a nebulous 'Balkan' Other (Razsa & Lindstrom, 2004, p. 639), dominant and alternative Slovenian cultural models both include Croatian music in their own Balkan referent, leading to juxtapositions on radio broadcasts and compilation albums which would be highly unlikely on their performers' home market. Croatian music's symbolic role in Slovenia is illustrated by a scene from Maja Weiss's film *Varuh meje* (Guardian of the frontier, 2001), in which three girls on a canoeing trip cross to the Croatian bank of the Kupa/Kolpa river and chorus, far from coincidentally, a hit by the Croatian star Severina entitled *'Djevojka sa sela'*—'Village girl'.

Political and cultural factors have therefore restricted the commercial opportunities for Croatian artists. Once performances 'across the border' in Serbia and Montenegro resumed, they were first met with an implicit political acceptability test, and more recently with media indifference. From the perspective of Croatian performers, transnational prospects have certainly improved but still do not match the conditions of federal Yugoslavia's integrated market. Yet, in light of recent technological advances in satellite television and internet communication, it might be argued that the entertainment market has undergone a qualitative transformation, and that a direct comparison between 1980s and contemporary music promotion is problematic.

Serbian and Other Ex-Yugoslav Musical Activity in Croatia

Even when most Croatian performers had become reconciled to viewing Serbia as another site of commercial operations, cultural flows in the opposite direction (Serbian performers in Croatia) remained contentious for longer. Before discussing this question in detail, it would be appropriate to consider activities by other republics' performers on the Croatian market. A handful of Slovenian schlager and dance artists have appeared on the Croatian market but left little impression, while the punk band Laibach retain their exclusive fanbase among a section of the urban rock audience, where their live performers' totalitarian references are understood as alternative art and as an opposite pole to the nationalist folk-rock which has emerged as a sub-genre of Croatian showbusiness (Glavan, 2002). Macedonian performers are all but absent from the Croatian scene, although Toše Proeski (already popular in Serbia) recorded an album for Croatia to capitalize on his appearance in the 2004 Eurovision Song Contest. The most active ex-Yugoslav performers in Croatia are unquestionably from Bosnia-Herzegovina, particularly the Bosniak singers Kemal Monteno, Dino Merlin and Hari Mata Hari,[10] and the Sarajevo band Zabranjeno pušenje.[11] In contrast, Boris Režak, the first Bosnian Serb singer to be launched in Croatia, experienced contractual difficulties with his 2004 album and struggled to achieve the exposure of his Bosniak counterparts (Jadrijević-Tomas, 2004). Neither have Bosniak artists been accepted by the Croatian music industry as fully equal participants: the 2001 award of several Porins (the annual Croatian music prize) to the Merlin-Ivana Banfić hit *'Godinama'* ('For years') prompted the ceremony's organizers, headed by Paolo Sfeci, to amend the regulations so that prizes could only be won by Croatian citizens (Oremović, 2002).

Industry resistance to ex-Yugoslav performers appearing in Croatia on equal terms may on one level be understood as a commercially protectionist response. Such a tactic would aim to maintain the privileged treatment enjoyed by early 1990s Croatian artists when other republics' artists were withdrawn from the state media and Croatian singers became insulated from potential Serbian competition. Indeed, critiques of contemporary Croatian popular music frequently allege that the artificial advantage encouraged complacency among music producers and elevated mediocre talents into national stars (e.g. Gall, 2000). The early 1990s' climate has been vividly described by Dubravka Ugrešić as an element of the Tudjmanist "confiscation of memory" immediately noticed in everyday life (Ugrešić, 1998, p. 228). This represented a deliberate strategy by the ruling Croatian Democratic Union (HDZ) to realign Croats' "symbolic universe" by removing from the historical and cultural spheres any reminder that Croatians had belonged to the national community of the former Yugoslav state: the political aim was to eliminate and stigmatize any allegiance other than to the regime which had secured Croatian independence (Zakošek, 2000, p. 110).

Purely commercial explanations therefore seem insufficient to account for the behaviour of industry professionals who had benefited throughout the 1990s from HDZ patronage. Both during and after the Tudjman era opposition to performances in Croatia by Serbian artists was led by Sfeci, whose continued loyalty to Tudjmanist ideology is suggested by his statement regarding a parliamentary proposal to liberalize the work-permit regime, claiming that it would be "excellent news for all Yugoslavs and regionalists" (Gatarić & Vuković, 2002). The Serbian musicians who 'returned' to Croatia under Tudjman were exclusively alternative rockers, including Rambo Amadeus (Vuković, 1998), and they first played in Istria and Rijeka, regions which have taken pride in multi-ethnicity and tolerance as a characteristic of their identity, to the extent that their inhabitants define themselves partially against other, less tolerant, Croats (Kalapoš, 2002, p. 84). Zagreb, then the only other venue for Serbian performances, was still understood as more likely to provoke an adverse reaction, or even violence, such as that against a 1996 Zabranjeno pušenje concert (Perić, 1996).

Croatian fans of Serbian artists often travelled to their Slovenian concerts instead, conferring on Slovenia a certain status as a liminal space for Croatian consumers of alternative cultural models. Djordje Balašević, among the most popular of them, was able to attract up to 10 000 Croatians to his frequent concerts in Ljubljana, Maribor and Portorož (Peršić, 2001). The prospect of a Balašević concert in Croatia only became conceivable after Tudjman's death, and occasioned intense speculation until the Slovenian supermarket chain Mercator assembled Balašević, Monteno, Oliver Dragojević (a respected Dalmatian *zabavna* singer) and Vlado Krušlin (of Slovenia) in December 2000 for two concerts in Sarajevo and Pula to mark new stores (Peršić, 2000). Balašević, whose pre-war popularity had been greatest in Croatia and Slovenia, performed his first solo concert in independent Croatia in June 2001 at the Pula Arena (Dobrila, 2001), and his first Zagreb concert in December 2002 (Pribačić & Mamić, 2002).

Between 2000 and 2002, however, announcements that Balašević might perform in Croatia met with public disapproval from music industry representatives, from certain journalists, and from Homeland War veterans' organizations.[12] These criticisms focused not only on Balašević's mid-1980s statements siding with Serbs against Kosovar Albanians (Jajčinović, 2002), but also on his early associations with the Yugoslav regime, particularly through his 1977 song '*Računajte na nas*' ('Count on us') which declared the younger generation's loyalty to Tito and the heritage of the Partisan movement (Gugo, 2000).[13] Yet Balašević's supporters too invested him with immense symbolic value, and anticipated his Croatian concerts "as a therapeutic séance and a symbolic beginning of a certain more civilized phase in Croatian–Serbian relations" (Gall, 2003b).

Typical in this respect were the words of Dražen Turina-Šajeta after the Mercator concert in Pula: Turina, himself a rock musician associated with Istria,[14] took it as a sign that "things are slowly coming back to normal", took note of audience members moved to tears, and wished that Sfeci and other opponents of Balašević "were there too to cry as well at the disintegration of their ideal" (Turina, 2000). One transnationalism theorist mentions in passing that "persons cannot be Yugoslavs when Yugoslavia is gone" (Berezin, 2003, p. 11). On the contrary, Balašević's fan-base may provide the clearest example of post-Yugoslav musical transnationalism: they manifest not only the "common identity" underpinning many transnational networks but the participation in "socio-cultural...activities" with which such networks are formed and perpetuated (Vertovec, 2001, p. 573). Indeed, one anthropologist's ex-Yugoslav informants experienced the former Yugoslavia as precisely "a cultural everyday space", composed of various collective rituals and cultural markers (Volčič, 2005, p. 15).

The major accusation against both Balašević and his fans was of 'Yugo-nostalgia': in Croatian political life, this concept had served as a catch-all insult for any individual or idea which failed to correspond to Tudjmanist ideology and which was therefore assumed self-evidently to prefer the inimical previous regime (Ugrešić, 1998, p. 231). The Croatian nationalist project, politically striving to emphasize its distance from the ideological structure it had replaced, denied any distinction between political and individual/generational nostalgia, and consciously encroached into private memory to demand overt rejection of any positive memories of common Yugoslav life (Drakulić, 1996, p. 147).

Before his 2001 Pula concert Balašević explicitly distinguished the "normal emotional human nostalgia" he was experiencing in Istria from the "nationalistic, territorial, or some Serbian or Yugoslav sense" with which a political nostalgic would mourn (Peršić, 2001). Similarly, Zlatko Gall, describing his own new-found appreciation of Balašević, wrote that such nostalgia was in no way subversive, "because emotional Yugo-nostalgia is completely legitimate...and because of the fundamental right to one's own and one's generation's past" (Gall, 2003b). In this emotional sense Balašević certainly figures as an embodiment of nostalgia, and appreciation for his music even offers a potential symbolic resource through which individual Croatians can express their distaste for the nationalist right's apparent monopolization of definitions of Croatian identity.

Serbian artists' performances in Croatia have frequently become a site of conflict where the limits of the Croatian cultural space are contested, and these debates have demonstrated the persistence of 1990s ideology in what is commonly thought of as the 'post-Tudjman' era (since 2000). The return of Serbian musicians has highlighted issues of private memory versus publicly displayed allegiance, and prompted Croatians to interrogate the politicized concept of nostalgia. At the same time the supposed post-Tudjman 'normalization' of Croatian cultural space suggests that one should re-examine the idea of transnationalism to account also for those whose displacement has been conceptual and temporal. The dynamics of the Balašević case, where the use of national–historical symbolism is particularly striking, invite a further study of the bases of musical preferences and Croatian identity.

Transnational Cultural Flows as Symbolic Resources

The coincidence of Balašević's 2001 concert with the summer of nationalist protests against General Mirko Norac's trial for war crimes (where the typical slogan on protestors' placards read 'We are all Mirko Norac') led fans from Split to travel to Pula with banners and T-shirts reading 'We are all Djordje Balašević' (Šarac & Jelaca, 2001).[15] Balašević has symbolic value on several grounds: his socio-musical position as a pop-rock singer who—apparently like much of his audience—disapproves of the dominance of newly composed folk music (Gordy, 1999, p. 107), his history of resistance to Milošević, which has become implicit in his performance persona, and his pre-existing role in the Croatian right-wing imagination as a symbol of ideological nostalgia. Combined, these criteria led him to be understood as an explicit site of resistance to the Norac protests' right-revanchism, and also to the emerging 'patriotic showbusiness' genre emerging from the commercial opportunities of this political climate.

Indeed, a fascinating aspect of musical transnationalism in Croatia is how the figures of artists from other republics function as symbolic markers to define variant interpretations of Croatian identity, as may be observed in the case of an August 2003 concert by Momčilo Bajagić-Bajaga. Bajaga's first concert in post-war Croatia, in the Istrian town of Labin, had passed peacefully (Žužić, 2002), but this Split concert (already rescheduled to avoid a clash with an HDZ Youth pre-election concert[16]) was cut short when tear-gas canisters were thrown into the open-air venue (Petranović, 2003c).

As a major Croatian city situated close to the Dinaric region of Herzegovina and Dalmatinska zagora (sources of much rural-to-urban migration during socialist industrialization), Split had had particularly sharp experience of the tensions associated with Titoist Yugoslavia's imperfect urbanization. Xavier Bougarel has pointed out that "forty years of accelerated modernization and urbanization have shifted the traditional antagonisms between [Yugoslav] town and countryside into the towns themselves" (Bougarel, 1999, p. 165). This discourse informs the anxieties of long-standing Split residents (including younger generations), in which Split and its familiar locales become public spaces contested by competing spatialized local identities.[17]

Particular sensitivity had been aroused by the nationalist singer Marko Perković Thompson's celebrated, or notorious, Split concert in August 2002. Miro Kučić, for instance, employed an essentialized conception of the Mediterranean on that occasion to underline how foreign such chauvinism was to Split's supposedly authentic nature, contrasting "the winds from the south", with "all their mildness and the beauty of the Mediterranean", with the recent arrival of "implacability, rudeness, [and] intolerance", carried on "the brutal, cold winds from Dinara" (Kučić, 2002). Accordingly, a Bajaga concert in Split took on added symbolic value as a re-affirmation of old-Split values against the nationalist Herzegovinan influx. Only two months earlier, in fact, one journalist from the Split daily *Slobodna Dalmacija* had expressed resentment of the fact that Serbian performers were avoiding Split "because it would be like pushing their hand into a hornet's nest when it doesn't want them there" (Ljubičić, 2003). The attack on Bajaga's concert was understood as also directed against "all those who—regardless of their place of birth—in Split today feel like the captives of other people's hate, xenophobia and primitivism" (Gall, 2003a). Coverage in the Rijeka-based *Novi list*, with a cosmopolitan urban readership, made exceptionally explicit use of the discourse when Zoran Krželj wrote that Split had thereby "once again stayed (or become) a village, that latest, backwoods Balkan [kind]" (Krželj, 2003).

The heavy-handed police treatment of victims, according to Krželj, provoked the crowd on a night of symbolic resistance into chanting the Električni orgazam song '*Igra rokenrol cela Jugoslavija*' ('All Yugoslavia is dancing rock-and-roll') (Krželj, 2003).[18] This prompted further reflections on the Tudjmanist and post-Tudjman Croatian state as institutionally chauvinist, and "gave added strength to the impression that this city is lost for the civilized, for that so-called silent, civic majority" (Petranović, 2003b). Another commentary described the incident as "the logical consequence of a decade in which a parallel history of Split has been told with hate speech". It mentioned the official blind eye turned to memorial masses for Ante Pavelić, a Split street named after the Ustaša ideologue Mile Budak, and Ustaša insignia displayed on the Riva (Gall, 2003a).

Bajaga's figure here represents different attitudes towards the desirable extent of Croatian relations with Serbia, but it also serves as a boundary-marker with which to construct and continually restate a variety of identities within Croatian society. To a certain number of urban Croatians, Serbian pop-rock and alternative performers exist as a cultural resource with which to distance themselves from musical genres they associate with the ruralization (and Herzegovinization) of Croatian city space, summed up by Boris Dežulović's comment that:

> The new Split audience has been recruited in large part from Herzegovina, from where there have come in the last ten years tens of thousands of new Splićani [inhabitants of Split] to whom narodnjaci [newly-composed folk songs] are some-what closer than Oliver Dragojević [a renowned singer from the city]. (Dežulović, 2002)

The Bajaga case demonstrates that these Croatians' established urban values may be expressed through a transnational identification as a mark of tolerance. Yet the transnational consumption of another musical genre, newly composed folk music, is associated in this discourse with the supposedly rural-in-urban population itself, providing an example of how identities can be shaped and reasserted through expressing value judgements in social interaction (see Jenkins, 1996, p. 4). The judgements of similarity and difference on which this method of identity-formation is founded depend on a community's "symbolic repertoire", with reference to which its members "suppose themselves to be more like each other than like the members of other communities" (Cohen, 1985, p. 21), and to which musical products may make a significant contribution (Edensor, 2002, p. 25). Urban-Croatian insecurity concerning rural-to-urban migration demands that Serbian *folk* singers' reception there should be considered separately from that of pop-rock stars.

The Transnationalism of Folk: Serbia, Croatia, Herzegovina

Unlike in the cases discussed above, the Zagreb concert in November 2004 of Željko Joksimović, the first large-scale performance given by a Serbian performer associated in Croatia with folk (Dervoz, 2004b),[19] attracted neither violent incidents nor antagonistic newspaper reports detailing the singer's politically connected past.[20] Coverage described a "euphoric", mainly young audience (Mamić, 2004), with the only discordant note being struck by the *Slobodna Dalmacija* reporter who employed an all too telling metaphor in concluding that the Serbian star was hoping "after the other neighbours, [to] subjugate the Croatian market too" (Marušić, 2004). Joksimović's arrival may represent a particularly significant development, since Serbian folk music has typically been marginalized—although far from absent—on the Croatian musical market.

Serbian folk artists were not promoted through the Croatian broadcast media (although TV Pink and the Karić Brothers channel are available to Croatian satellite-TV subscribers), although they were occasionally profiled in print (e.g. Strukar, 2003a). Their recordings were not sold in mainstream outlets, and were mainly available through pirate vendors. Vesna Zmijanac estimated that some of her records had sold up to 40 000 copies in Croatia in pirate editions (Šćepanović, 2003),[21] while a 1995 investigation suggested similar figures for Zmijanac, Dragana Mirković and Lepa Brena, and noted that "even the hated Ceca" (the widow of the assassinated paramilitary commander Željko Ražnato-vić-Arkan) had sold 18 000 pirate cassettes (Djilas, 1996). Such figures, in a market where sales of 10 000 copies could be a rarity (Gall, 2000), were of some anxiety to the Croatian music industry as part of its concern with piracy in general. Folk concerts predominantly took place in small clubs and bars, particularly the Ludnica and Od sumraka do zore/Pasha discotheques in Zagreb, Oks in Osijek, and several venues in Split. Even in 1990 venues in Zagreb playing newly composed folk music had already enjoyed underground popularity, thanks to their appeal as a culturally illicit form of entertainment (Rasmussen, 2002, pp. 184–185), and this again appears to be the case in post-Tudjman Croatia.

However, Serbian folk singers' concerts normally occurred below the threshold of media attention, apart from during a spring 2002 edition of the talk-show *Latinica*, which dealt with the subject and featured the Serbian folk singer Miroslav Ilić on his first post-war tour of Croatia (Stanivuković, 2002). A November 2004 survey for the Croa-tian daily *Večernji list* revealed the number of small-scale appearances by artists including Ilić, Neda Ukraden and Dragan Kojić-Keba, with Zmijanac accumulating the most per-formances (Dervoz, 2004a). Ceca Ražnatović's associations with Milošević, and with the events surrounding the death in 2003 of the Serbian prime minister Zoran Djindjić (Greenberg, 2006, p. 142), continue to make her perceived as unsuitable to perform in Croatia. Nonetheless, she too enjoys an underground following, supposedly so much so that the image of nationalist Croats hypocritically blasting Ceca's music from their cars has become a cliché of Croatian discourse (Ljubičić, 2003; Gall, 2002b; Petranović, 2003a). Nonetheless, this image's very frequency suggests that it may be underpinned by symbolically based social value judgements—which frown upon such overtly dis-played nationalism by aligning it with this 'most Serbian', most Othered, Serbian performer.

Joksimović, however, transcended this framework after attaining high levels of recog-nition among the Croatian audience with his second place in the 2004 Eurovision Song Contest—helped by maximum points from the Croatian public 'televote'. The entirely unexpected result occasioned much comment both in Croatia and in the Serbian press (Trajković, 2004), and paved the way for Joksimović's Zagreb performance,[22] when one headline observed that he had "opened the borders to ex-Yu music" (Mikac, 2004). In 2004 it remained too early to assess whether Joksimović had done so. Concerts by Serbian artists including Bajaga, Balašević, Zdravko Čolić, Dragana Mirković and Indira Radić took place thereafter in Croatia amid little media comment, suggesting that they were no longer a notorious novelty—especially when they were by pop-rock or *zabavna* stars rather than folk performers. Even the appearance of Lepa Brena, the most emblematic newly composed folk singer of socialist Yugoslavia (Ugrešić, 1998, p. 231), on Alka Vuica's television talk-show *Jedan na jedan* in early 2005 failed to ignite the reactions which surrounded Balašević's return to Croatia. Yet the same could not be said for Petar Vlahov's January 2005 interview with Ceca Ražnatović, which pro-voked so many complaints that the show was never even broadcast (Mamić, 2005). Appar-ently Ceca's unsuitability extended even to representing her in the discourse of showbusiness personality rather than in that of wartime and political guilt. In this instance, at least, the boundaries of the Croatian cultural space are being consistently marked by excluding Ražnatović and her ethnopolitical connotations.

Another transnational musical product also figures strongly in the Croatian symbolic repertoire: music performed by certain Bosnian Croat singers, and especially those who have associated themselves with the post-Tudjman sub-genre of patriotically themed showbusiness. It is debatable whether this interaction should even be treated as trans-nationalism: although the flow takes place across a political border, these artists would emphasize the cultural unity of their Croatian and Herzegovinan-Croat audience and make the case that the border is artificial. Performers of Croatian and Bosnian-Croat origin have equal standing in this emerging genre, as their music also indicates. For example, that of Marko Perković Thompson (from Čavoglave in Croatia) recognizes Herzegovina (or 'Herceg-Bosna') as an integral component of the Croatian landscape. In 2002 the Croatian Democratic Union of Bosnia-Herzegovina (HDZ-BiH) engaged Thompson for their climactic election rallies, and even adopted a line from his song '*E, moj narode*' ('O, my people') as one of their slogans (Bubalo, 2002).[23]

Bosnian Croats who have entered the Croatian discographic market from this background include Tiho Orlić (from Mostar) and Mate Bulić, a folk singer among the most popular artists in the Croat diaspora (Senjković & Dukić, 2005, p. 50). The chauvinistic attitudes which some of them continue to express on- and off-stage remind one that transnational activity is by no means necessarily associated with reconciliation between the successor states.[24] Another prominent Bosnian Croat singer, Ivan Mikulić, performed *zabavna* music but belonged to patriotic showbusiness by participating in right-wing events and concerts.[25] When Mikulić won the 2004 *Dora* festival and the opportunity to perform at the Eurovision Song Contest, a journalist from *Novi list* (a Rijeka daily) concluded with disapproval that "Ivan Mikulić…has quickly acquired the nickname in Rijeka of a soft Marko Perković Thompson" (Brajčić, 2004). As became evident in the discussions of local identity in Split, the discourses surrounding Thompson himself are an even more acute example of many urban Croats' ambivalence to cultural markers associated with the Dinara region transected by the Croatian–Bosnian border.

Thompson has consistently embraced 'Dinaric' musical signifiers, and indeed his style has become paradoxically characterized by the Macedonian-style 7/8 beat first incorporated into rock music by Goran Bregović's Bijelo dugme (Gall, 2002a). Niko Bete's song '*Mirko Norac*', dedicated to the general indicted for war crimes, is likewise set to the 7/8 rhythm.[26] Following the violence against Zabranjeno pušenje in 1996, Paolo Sfeci had stated that the incident had "only shown that there is no place for the eastern [*istočnjački*] melos in Croatia!" (Perić, 1996). In some right-wing imaginaries, however, such antagonism can be waived to accommodate these hyper-patriotic artists—or, as Zlatko Gall memorably commented, "what if his [Thompson's] musical expression verges on Balkan turbofolk, if he's a turbo-Croat?" (Gall, 2002b).

Anthony Cohen speculates that "structural forms" appropriated from elsewhere may still "become new vehicles for the expressions of indigenous meanings", and even "for the reassertion and symbolic expression of the community's boundaries" (Cohen, 1985, p. 37), and this would appear to hold true for Thompson and Bete. However, the suffusion of anti-patriotic showbusiness discourses with a wider Croatian ambivalence towards newly composed folk music and so-called 'eastern' musical elements leads one to reflect on a deeper level at which transnational flows have operated in the post-Yugoslav environment: the supposed influence of Serbian showbusiness-folk on Croatian musical production.

Showbusiness Folk Music as a Transnational Form

Serbian performers, as noted in the first sections of this paper, were subject to hostility and setbacks in 1990s Croatia: yet, even then, the popularity of newly composed folk music (NCFM) could be said to have been sustained, or even increased. In the Yugoslav era this genre had mainly been associated with Serbia and Bosnia (Rasmussen, 2002, p. 95). During the 1990s, however, certain techniques from NCFM became apparent in Croatian pop production, a development which was viewed by certain professional critics and musicians as transgressing the boundaries of musically expressed Croatian identity. The approaches taken towards folk-influenced *zabavna* music and its apparent 'eastern melos' indicate how the transnational phenomenon of showbusiness-folk was incorporated or denied as an element of Croatian cultural space.

During the 1980s the use of electronic instrumentation and pop-style promotion in newly composed folk music had culminated in the repertoire of performers such as Lepa Brena. Brena based herself in Serbia after the disintegration of Yugoslavia and, along with her colleagues, was then excluded from the Croatian market. One Croatian ethnomusicologist takes pains to emphasize that NCFM was not an established Croatian genre before 1991 (or, implicitly, afterwards), noting instead Croatia's affinity to *zabavna* music, tamburica-pop,[27] and "Anglo-American-style pop and rock" (Ceribašić, 2000, pp. 227–228). Yet, even though NCFM was mainly released by other republics' record companies, a Croatian audience still existed, and individual Croatian producers had begun to experiment with the so-called 'eastern melos' even in the 1980s. They included Tonči Huljić and his band Magazin (not least on their mid-1980s hit 'Istambul'), while Doris Dragović recorded several songs for her 1989 album '*Budi se dan*' which employed NCFM's characteristic tremolo vocal technique. Rajko Dujmić, producer of the Novi fosili group, at the time viewed his collaboration with Neda Ukraden (a Bosnian Serb singer from Sarajevo) as "a pioneering attempt to introduce the folk sound into pop music" (Luković, 1989, p. 277).

Thus the Croatian fusion of *zabavna* schlager with NCFM elements was not, as some critiques imply, concocted from nothing after Croatia's independence. Nonetheless, it gathered greater pace in the 1990s, when it was proverbially epitomized by Huljić, Magazin and the clients of his record-label Tonika. Other performers, such as Severina or Ivana Banfić, came to include increasing proportions of this music in their repertoires, and the genre in turn fused with others, especially with dance in the work of the groups Colonia and Karma.[28] These songs incorporate folk-style rhythms and vocal ululation while retaining some degree of *zabavna* orchestration or melody, while the synthesized accordion flourishes common to the Serbian variant are not present in Croatian repertoires. Their lyrics, meanwhile, operate like those of Serbian/Bosnian NCFM by relying on "clichéd syntagms and rhymes" and melodramatic situations which, combined with repetitive melodies, work to make them as memorable as possible (Dragićević-Šešić, 1994, pp. 205–206) or to convey images of romantic and family life (Čolović, 1985, pp. 185–186).

The most frequent Croatian critique of this trend directly connects it with the early 1990s, arguing that the removal of Serbian cultural products from the media created a commercial opportunity to fulfil consumers' demands by providing a new stable of artists whose 'Croatianness' was not in question, and who would perform "pseudo-folkloric schlager" to replace "its 'newly-composed' aesthetic eastern relative" (Gall, 2000). An extreme example of this ambivalence is given in an anecdote retold by Dubravka Ugrešić, who writes that an unknown Croatian female singer re-recorded a number of songs by Neda Ukraden (by then living in Serbia)—ostensibly to return the work of Ukraden's Croatian songwriters to "the corpus of Croatian pop" (Ugrešić, 1998, pp. 140–141), but perhaps also as another attempt to turn Croatians' ambiguous relationship with *narodnjaci* to commercial advantage.

However, the pre-1991 origins of Croatian *narodnjaci* invite a deeper examination of Croatian discourses, where Serbian 'turbofolk' can operate as a convenient benchmark against which to judge the 'cheapest' Croatian specimens. Serbian folk music itself is usually abbreviated into the figures of Ceca Ražnatović (made all the more suitable to represent the Other by virtue of her marriage to Željko Ražnatović-Arkan)[29] or by Lepa Brena; other showbusiness-folk stars, such as Jelena Karleuša or Dragana Mirković, do not figure in this symbolism. The strength of Ceca's associations with the Milošević regime, and of Brena's with the previous one, suggest that the decisive indicators in these value-judgements are non-musical—and that a Croatian cultural identity is being implicitly defined with reference to its supposed political opposites.

Nonetheless, Croatian *narodnjaci* (folk-type songs) are less likely to be criticized as '*srpski*' ('Serb') or '*jugoslovenski*' ('Yugoslav') than as '*istočnjački*' ('Eastern'). This framework is rooted in the 'symbolic geography' identified by Milica Bakić-Hayden and Robert Hayden, where a nation's particular Other is constructed as non-European and 'Balkan' (Bakić-Hayden & Hayden, 1992, p. 10; see also Razsa & Lindstrom, 2004). The music critic of the Croatian daily *Jutarnji list* provided a striking example of this when commenting on a rumoured collaboration between Željko Joksimović and Ivana Banfić. Croatian showbusiness had, apparently, "been 'Serbianised' [*posrbila*], i.e. Turkicised [*poturčila*], a long time ago" even without that duet, and it was impossible to think that "Colonia, Thompson, [Miroslav] Škoro, Mate Bulić or Magazin are autochthonous Croatian products". Continuing the eastern-related symbolism, the clients of Tonči Huljić were described as renegades or "*poturice*", a word connoting Christian converts to Islam during the wars with the Ottoman Empire (Dragaš, 2004). Even when these allusions are employed as a knowing metaphor, the inherent symbolism remains highly significant.

If international popular music styles in Croatia enable a sense of belonging to a global community (Kalapoš, 2002, p. 90), much of the unease surrounding the folk-based turn in Croatian music may involve a perception that it connects national culture to a more limited 'Balkan' community and to the ruralized urban culture from which NCFM originated (Rasmussen, 2002, p. 200). Describing Serbian music, Eric Gordy understands the folk element of Serbian 'turbofolk' as primarily a "sociological" category, where folk is constructed according to "other basic social oppositions: the urban against the rural and semi-urban publics, and as a parallel, rock and roll against folk" (Gordy, 1999, pp. 135–136). In the same vein, Milena Dragićević-Šešić describes NCFM as enabling "a person with a traditional structure of thought and feeling [who] otherwise feels alienated and rejected" in the city to relieve their alienation with a musical product which corresponds to that familiar, traditional structure, despite its modern or even exotic orchestration (Dragićević-Šešić 1994, p. 57). If NCFM provides a means for its listeners to escape full submission to the values of the city—and its opponents certainly appear to understand it thus—then unease about its popularity may ultimately imply anxiety for the universalism, or otherwise, of individual consciousness in Croatian society.

In terms of politics Dunja Rihtman-Auguštin considered that the use of nationalism as a form of political mobilization in the 1980s had particular resonance for "the semi-urban suburbs [and]. . .newly-settled residents of the centre", for whom the nation provided a framework which could connect a new and somewhat alien city identity to a more familiar local identity (Rihtman-Auguštin, 2000, pp. 29–30). If it could be established that both musical producers and nationalist politicians were striving for the same target audience, there would be even more reason to investigate any harmony of thought or action between the music industry and political ideology in Croatia.

In terms of showbusiness, meanwhile, the argument that Croatian folk-type music only exists as a substitute for an authentic Serbian product has become even harder to substantiate now that younger stars have emerged whose target audience might not even have been born when the war in Croatia finished. Instead, *narodnjaci* appear to have an established place in Croatian popular music, as shown by the career of Severina Vučković, who became Croatia's most prominent female singer in precisely this period. Severina has received criticism for performing little but a "sequence of orthodox eastern [*istočnjački*] turbofolk themes", which positions her as "a Lijepa Brijena", i.e. an acceptably Croatian version of Lepa Brena (Gall, 2001b). Brena and Severina emerged under quite different social circumstances, but both artists have resorted to similar methods in their use of multiple stage personae,[30] a technique which has taken Severina from her 1993 album '*Dalmatinka*' ('Dalmatian woman'), to her 1998 album '*Djevojka sa sela*' ('Village girl'), and finally to her late-2004 single '*Hrvatica*' ('Croatian woman').[31] Positively or negatively, Brena exists as a cultural pattern within which Severina could be understood inside and outside Croatia, even if she does not deliberately strive to conform to it.

Although the national narratives of the former Yugoslav communities have altered since the late 1980s, musical preferences have to a certain degree endured, and the market has responded accordingly. While the 1990s ideologues of independent Croatia officially endeavoured to distance the Croatian people from their Balkan neighbours, a state-favoured music industry nonetheless allowed performers of the transnational genre of *narodnjaci* to flourish to such an extent that, since Severina's high-profile Croatian and Bosnian concert tour in 2001–02, Croatia has essentially re-exported a folk-pop star to all the other successor states as one of the most iconic singers on the territory of former Yugoslavia.

Conclusion

Now that artists such as Joksimović and Severina understand their audience in transnational terms, it might be tempting to conclude that the popular music market of former Yugoslavia is turning full circle and repairing the trans-republican linkages interrupted by the consequences of disintegration. Anti-nationalist dissent has emphasized the persistence of personal memory throughout this process, implying the extent of resistance in the private sphere even when nationalizing projects are complied with in public (e.g. Drakulić, 1996) and suggesting in passing that popular music is intimately related to this sphere of the everyday (Ugrešić, 1998, p. 133).[32] From this perspective it might be comforting to interpret the recent rapid growth of transnational consumption and production in ex-Yugoslav popular music as the repair of formerly shared experiences. Yet this would overlook the effect of Croatia's 1990s severance from Yugoslav cultural space, when Croatian musicians and consumers nonetheless confirmed their affinity for the transnational form of newly composed folk music. In the late 1980s Croatia's most successful musical exports to the rest of Yugoslavia had predominantly been *zabavna* performers such as Dragojević, Dragović, Novi fosili, Magazin and Tereza Kesovija (Dragićević-Šešić, 1994, p. 106). These personalities have retained their popularity, but they have been joined (even outstripped?) by performers whose music approaches showbusiness-folk.

At the same time music from the Yugoslav period, which suddenly became transnational, has also taken on new meanings in the identity narratives of younger generations, where the "Yugoslav imaginary" is indivisible from the "unique, culturally specific brand of rock'n'-roll" produced in socialist Yugoslavia and the bands of the 1980s rock scene are conceptualized as "the cultural links between different [Yugoslav] nations" (Volčič, forthcoming, pp. 17–18). This orientation does not hold true for all youth. Indeed, the 'moral panics' which have ensued on the topic of Croatian teenagers listening to (Serbian) newly composed folk or (Croatian) patriotic music (Perasović, 2006, p. 5) suggest that the symbolic opposition of 'folk' and 'rock' (Prica, 1991; Gordy, 1999) has persisted into post-Yugoslav youth cultures. In the case of 1980s Yugoslav rock it is uncertain how often its consumption may serve as a generational mark of difference in cases where adolescents' parents are of an age to have participated in the 'new wave' scene themselves. Yet, as the cases of Balašević's and Bajaga's return to Croatia indicate, it certainly appears to serve as a *social* mark of difference which distinguishes one's own group from others of a perceived less-than-urban background who are imagined as consumers of transnational *folk* music.

In 2005 and 2006 the publicizing and commodification of transnational products from the Yugoslav period reached a state where "the Yugoslav past" became "one more free-floating signifier of consumer desire", as in the widely mediatized reunion of the iconic ex-Yugoslav band Bijelo dugme (Volčič, forthcoming, p. 4). New musical products could be devised which played with those transnational signifiers in a "recycling" of past identities (Mikić, 2006, pp. 6–7). Simultaneously post-Yugoslav transnational music penetrated ex-domestic markets with ever more visibility, assisted by the cross-border reach of the internet and satellite television: MTV Adria promoting 'urban' music and TV Pink transmitting showbusiness-folk. However, these developments depended on the negotiation of political and cultural obstacles which had been put in place between 1999 and 2004, a time of reconstruction and re-contextualization in ex-Yugoslav cultural spaces. Moreover, the tensions of identity observed during this earlier period were by no means resolved, but continued to affect the reception of transnational music despite the opening-up of national media spaces.

Acknowledgements

Some research for this paper was enabled by the Arts and Humanities Research Council. I am grateful to Ana Dević, Jasna Dragović-Soso, Denisa Kostovicova, Jelena Obradović, Obrad Savić, Claire Wilkinson, Daphne Winland and anonymous reviewers for comments on earlier versions of this paper.

Notes

1. *Schlager* is a central and northern European style of popular music typically featuring romantic and sentimental lyrical themes and orchestral or electric-guitar musical arrangements. Ex-Yugoslav *zabavna*

(light-entertainment) music also includes elements of Italian *canzonetta*, and in stricter senses excludes so-called 'newly composed folk music', which is classified as *folk* or *narodna*.

2. Varešanović and Džinović are Bosnian performers; Nikolić is Serbian.

3. Sfeci was formerly a member of the rock group Boa.

4. Emblematic of Vuica's repertoire, also including versions of songs by Bijelo dugme and Momčilo Bajagić-Bajaga, is her 2004 song '*Bosna*' ('Bosnia'), a duet with the folk singer Halid Bešlić and una-shamedly nostalgic for 1980s multi-ethnic Sarajevo.

5. See Razsa and Lindstrom (2004).

6. On 'rock discourse', see Frith (1996, p. 67).

7. The fact that Oliver Dragojević, an iconic Dalmatian *zabavna* singer, has not yet performed in Serbia has also been interpreted in the Croatian and Serbian media as a refusal to do so. If this is the case, his refusal has been less public than Giuliano's or Kovač's.

8. TV Pink's owner, Željko Mitrović, also owns the Serbian company City Records, which releases the largest amount of Croatian music under licence (*Globus*, 2005).

9. Is the Slovene nation here permanently defined not by its separateness, but by the act of *having* separated?

10. The most successful releases by mainstream Bosniak artists are often duets with Croatian female singers, such as Monteno/Danijela Martinović (2001), Leo/Severina (2000), Merlin/Ivana Banfić (2000), Merlin/Nina Badrić (2004), and Hari Mata Hari/Banfić (2003). This almost suggests that they are most commercially acceptable when symbolically 'vouched for' by a Croatian partner.

11. Zabranjeno pušenje split during the war in Bosnia, leading to Bosnian-based and Serbian-based versions of the band (the Serbian-based version, founded by Nele Karajlić) is also known as the No Smoking Orchestra). The band active in Croatia is the Bosnian branch.

12. For example, the veterans who protested against Balašević using the Croatian National Theatre for a concert in Osijek (Stojčić, 2002)

13. In 2002 Balašević claimed that he stopped performing '*Računajte na nas*' ('Count on us') in 1983 or 1984 after he was personally required to sing it at a state celebration by the federal interior minister, Stane Dolanc (Stanić, 2002).

14. On Turina's relationship to Istrian and Croatian identities, see Kalapoš (2002, pp. 68–74).

15. Split had been the site of the largest pro-Norac demonstrations.

16. Apparently at Bajaga's insistence.

17. Similar dynamics in Belgrade have been described by Eric Gordy (1999, pp. 105–108) and Zala Volčić (2005, pp. 648–650). On spatialized identity in general, see Edensor, 2002, p. 48.

18. In Zala Volčić's interviews with young Slovenian and Macedonian intellectuals on the memory of Yugoslavia, "almost all" her informants recalled and sang this song (Volčić, forthcoming, p. 17).

19. Between 5000 and 6500 people attended Zagreb's Dom sportova. Joksimović is marketed in Serbia as a singer of pop, not folk, music; in Croatia, however, he is received as another folk singer.

20. Despite one journalist's attempt in May to call scandalous attention to Joksimović's statement to TV Pink that he would "conquer Constantinople" at Eurovision (Strukar, 2004).

21. The figure may have related to pre-war releases.

22. In the meantime, Joksimović had also become the first Serbian artist to submit a song (performed by Alka Vuica) to Croatia's Splitski festival.

23. The party had previously relied on *zabavna* singer Tereza Kesovija and rock singer Jura Stublić. In 2002 Ivana Banfić, Mišo Kovač and Crvena jabuka were engaged for NS-RB election meetings, while Vesna Zmijanac and Miroslav Ilić performed for Bosnian Serb parties.

24. The ex-Yugoslav diaspora provides other examples of transnationalism without reconciliation (e.g. the YugoUK Internet forum which carries pro-Milošević, anti-Croatian newsfeeds on its front page (http://www.yugouk.co.uk, accessed 29 May 2006)) but is still happy to promote Croatian performers including Magazin and Darko Rundek in its concert listings. On ex-Yugoslav popular music and identity among migrants in Vienna, see Fischer (2005, pp. 67–71).

25. These include performing at the 2003 Sinj Alka (jousting festival), and appearing in a video honouring Tudjman during the overture at Thompson's 2002 concerts (Paštar, 2003; Gospodnetić, 2002).

26. Since the song's release, Norac has been convicted of war crimes by a Croatian court.

27. The *tamburica* is a stringed instrument from Slavonia.

28. In Serbia 'turbo folk' likewise came to overlap with dance (Kronja, 2001, pp. 66–7).

29. For instance, Krželj (2002), Gall (2002b), Dežulović (2002) Vodopija (2004) and Pavičić (2005).

30. On Brena, see Dragićević-Šešić (1994, pp. 146–147).
31. Compare Brena's '*Jugoslovenka*' ('Yugoslav woman'). In fact, the Croatian performer most open to comparisons with Brena in this period was perhaps Maja Šuput, who made great use of Brena's characteristic male backing-vocals and her typical lyrical themes of joy and entertainment—and was criticized on these grounds from a 'Balkanist' perspective (Strukar & Mamić, 2003).
32. On ethnological approaches to the reproduction of national (etc.) symbols in everyday life, see Kalapoš (2002, pp. 11–12).

References

Bakić-Hayden, M. & Hayden, R. M. (1992) Orientalist variations on the theme 'Balkans': symbolic geography in recent Yugoslav cultural politics, *Slavic Review*, 51(1), pp. 1–15.

Berezin, M. (2003) *Europe Without Borders: Remapping Territory, Citizenship, and Identity in a Transnational Age* (Baltimore, MD: Johns Hopkins University Press).

Blažević, D. (2004) Pjevat ću besplatno Jadranki Kosor u predsjedničkoj kampanji, *Slobodna Dalmacija*, 20 June.

Bougarel, X. (1999) Yugoslav wars: the 'revenge of the countryside' between sociological reality and nationalist myth, *East European Quarterly*, 33(2), pp. 157–175.

Brajčić, S. (2004) Mikulić za razliku od većine bar zna pjevati, *Novi list*, 16 March.

Bubalo, R. (2002) U predizbornu utrku u BiH uključene brojne zvijezde hrvatske i srpske glazbene estrade, *Večernji list*, 21 September.

Ceribašić, N. (2000) Defining women and men in the context of war: images in Croatian popular music in the 1990s, in: P. Moisala & B. Diamond (Eds), *Music and Gender* (Urbana, IL: University of Illinois Press).

Cohen, A. P. (1985) *The Symbolic Construction of Community* (London: Routledge).

Čolović, I. (1985) *Divlja književnost: etnolingvističko proučavanje paraliterature* (Belgrade: Nolit).

Dervoz, L. (2004a) Srpski folk u Lijepoj naši, *Večernji list*, 4 October.

Dervoz, L. (2004b) Željko Joksimović bacio Zagreb u trans, *Večernji list*, 4 November.

Dežulović, B. (2002) Kraljica Marakane u Slobodnoj Dalmaciji, *Dani*, 5 July.

Djilas, M. (1996) Daj nešto za plakanje, *NIN*, 20 September.

Djilas, M. (1999) Pjevači na granici, *AIM*, 22 December, available online at: http://www.aimpress.ch/dyn/pubs/archive/data/199912/91222-008-pubs-zag.htm, accessed 30 July 2004.

Dobrila, D. (2001) Kao stari gladijator vraćam se u Arenu, *Novi list*, 18 June.

Dragaš, A. (2004) 'Balkanizacija' hrvatske estrade, *Jutarnji list*, 16 July.

Dragićević-Šešić, M. (1994) *Neofolk kultura: publika i njene zvezde* (Sremski Karlovci: Izdavačka knjižarnica Zorana Stojanovića).

Drakulić, S. (1996) *Café Europa: Life after Communism* (London: Abacus).

Edensor, T. (2002) *National Identity, Popular Culture and Everyday Life* (Oxford: Berg).

Faist, T. (2000) Transnationalization in international migration: implications for the study of citizenship and culture, *Ethnic and Racial Studies*, 23(2), pp. 189–222.

Fischer, W. (2005) A polyphony of belongings: (turbo) folk, power, and migrants, in: T. Marković & V. Mikić (Eds), *Music and Networking*, pp. 58–71 (Belgrade: Signature).

Fiske, J. (1987) *Television Culture* (London: Routledge).

Frith, S. (1996) *Performing Rites: On the Value of Popular Music* (Cambridge: Cambridge University Press).

Gall, Z. (2000) Nadgrobne ploče, *Feral tribune*, 755.

Gall, Z. (2001a) Ljuta trava zaborava, *Slobodna Dalmacija*, 29 November.

Gall, Z. (2001b) Prianja baš uz svaku podlogu, *Slobodna Dalmacija*, 3 December.

Gall, Z. (2002a) Neću u Čavoglave, nisam ni prije!, *Slobodna Dalmacija*, 28 August.

Gall, Z. (2002b) Thompson: Hrvatska Ceca, *Slobodna Dalmacija*, 21 September.

Gall, Z. (2003a) Pljuni i zaplači, moja Croatio, *Slobodna Dalmacija*, 13 August.

Gall, Z. (2003b) Povrat Djoletove imovine, *Slobodna Dalmacija*, 5 February.

Gatarić, Lj. & Ž. Vuković (2002) Strani pjevači i strojari 30 dana bez radne dozvole, *Večernji list*, 10 June.

Glavan, D. (2002) Kratka povijest ekstremne rock-ikonografije, *Večernji list*, 12 October.

Globus (2005) Prvi čovjek TV Pinka—Željko Mitrović, 7 January.

Gordy, E. D. (1999) *The Culture of Power in Serbia: Nationalism and the Destruction of Alternatives* (University Park, PA: Pennsylvania State University Press).

Goreta, M. (2002) Žao mi je što ne mogu Ponoviti Velike koncerte, *Jutarnji list*, 8 March. (Note haceks on Z in Žao and s in što.)

Gospodnetić, L. (2002) Thompson i Hrvati, *Slobodna Dalmacija*, 17 September.

Greenberg, J. (2006) "Goodbye Serbian Kennedy": Zoran Đinđić and the new democratic masculinity in Serbia, *East European Politics and Societies*, 20(1), pp. 126–151.

Grujičić, N. (2000) Povlašćeni odmetnici, *Vreme*, 14 December.

Gugo, Λ. (2000) Djoka, ne računaj na nas!, *Slobodna Dalmacija*, 30 July.

Hannerz, U. (1996) *Transnational Connections: Culture, People, Places* (London: Routledge).

Jackson, P., Crang, P. & Dwyer, C. (2004) The spaces of transnationality, in: P. Jackson, P. Crang & C. Dwyer (Eds), *Transnational Spaces* (London: Routledge).

Jadrijević-Tomas, S. (2004) Nisu ga htjeli Croatia Records ni Radijski festival, *Slobodna Dalmacija*, 5 July.

Jajčinović, M. (2002) Tko to tamo gostuje, *Večernji list*, 22 December.

Jenkins, R. (1996) *Social Identity* (London: Routledge).

Kalapoš, S. (2002) *Rock po istrijanski: o popularnoj kulturi, regiji i identiteta* (Zagreb: Naklada Jesenski i Turk).

Kellner, D. (1995) *Media Culture: Cultural Studies, Identity and Politics between the Modern and the Postmodern* (London: Routledge).

Kiossev, A. (2002) The dark intimacy: maps, identities, acts of identification, in: D. Bjelić & O. Savić (Eds), *Balkan as Metaphor: Between Globalisation and Fragmentation* (London: MIT Press).

Kronja, I. (2001) *Smrtonosni sjaj: masovna psihologija i estetika turbo-folka* (Belgrade: Tehnokratia).

Krželj, Z. (2002) Norac i Gotovina nisu došli, ali svi ostali jesu!, *Novi list*, 17 September.

Krželj, Z. (2003) Bajagin koncert prekinut bombama sa suzavcem, *Novi list*, 13 August.

Kučić, M. (2002) Surovi vjetar s Dinare, *Slobodna Dalmacija*, 8 October.

Lacko, R. (1999) Na poziv don Branka Sbutege pjevat ću u Herceg Novom, *Večernji list*, 16 December.

Laušević, M. (2000) Some aspects of music and politics in Bosnia, in: J. M. Halpern & D. A. Kideckel (Eds), *Neighbours at War: Anthropological Perspectives on Yugoslav Ethnicity, Culture and History* (University Park, PA: Pennsylvania State University Press).

Ljubičić, S. (2003) Srpski pjevači boje se Splita, *Slobodna Dalmacija*, 2 June.

Luković, P. (1989) *Bolja prošlost: prizori iz muzičkog života Jugoslavije* (Belgrade: Mladost).

Mamić, Z. (2004) Željko Joksimović zahvalio Hrvatima na '12 poena', *Novi list*, 5 November.

Mamić, Z. (2005) Vlahovu zbog Ceca prijetili smrću, Novoj TV bombom, *Novi list*, 28 January.

Marinović, M. (2001) Još je prerano da pjevam u Srbiji, a oni se zabavljaju, *Večernji list*, 7 December.

Marušić, A. (2004) Joksimović se stekao, tinejdžerice ludovale, *Slobodna Dalmacija*, 5 November.

Mikac, N. (2004) Joksimović otvorio granice ex-Yu glazbi, *Večernji list*, 5 November.

Mikić, V. (2006) The way we (just me, myself and I) were: recycling (national) identities in recent popular music, paper presented at the conference on 'Musical Culture and Memory', University of Arts, Belgrade, 12–14 April.

Oremović, A. (2002) Porin potiho strahuje od Huljićeva bojkotiranja s Croatijom Records, *Večernji list*, 11 January.

Paštar, T. (2003) Cetinjani iščekuju Norčev povratak, *Slobodna Dalmacija*, 2 February.

Pavičić, J. (2005) Spoj kiča i katolicizma, *Jutarnji list*, 12 March.

Perasović, B. (2006) Youth, the media, and subculture in post-socialist societies, paper presented at the RIME Workshop, Subotica, 11–13 May.

Perić, G. (1996) Pušenje zbog Zabranjenog pušenja, *AIM*, 27 April, available online at: http://www.aimpress.ch/dyn/pubs/archive/data/199604/60427-001-pubs-zag.htm, accessed 30 July 2004.

Peršić, V. (2000) Polemike i dvojbe uz prvi nastup Djordje Balaševića u samostalnoj Hrvatskoj, *Novi list*, 1 December.

Peršić, V. (2001) Mene hrvatska publika razumije i bez 'titlovanja', *Novi list*, 8 June.

Petranović, D. (2003a) Dokazivanje hrvatstva, *Slobodna Dalmacija*, 13 August.

Petranović, D. (2003b) Sezona suzavca, *Slobodna Dalmacija*, 14–15 August.

Petranović, D. (2003c) Suzavac rasplakao Bajagu i Bačvice, *Slobodna Dalmacija*, 13 August.

Portes, A., Guarnizo, L. E. & Landolt, P. (1999) The study of transnationalism: pitfalls and promise of an emergent research field, *Ethnic and Racial Studies*, 22(2), pp. 217–237.

Pribačić, D. & Mamić, Z. (2002) I najbezazlenija riječ ima preveliku težinu, *Novi list*, 15 December.

Prica, I. (1991) *Omladinska potkultura u Beogradu: simbolička praksa* (Belgrade: Etnografski institute SANU).

Prica, I. (1993) Notes on everyday life in war, in: L. Čale Feldman, I. Prica & R. Senjković (Eds), *Fear, Death and Resistance: An Ethnography of War: Croatia 1991–1992* (Zagreb: Institute of Ethnology and Folklore Research).

Rašević, M. (2005) MTV-jeva audicija 24, travnja u Splitu, *Slobodna Dalmacija*, 31 March.

Rasmussen, Lj. V. (2002) *Newly-Composed Folk Music of Yugoslavia* (London: Routledge).

Razsa, M. & Lindstrom, N. (2004) Balkan is beautiful: Balkanism in the political discourse of Tuđman's Croatia, *East European Politics and Societies*, 18(4), pp. 628–650.

Rihtman-Auguštin, D. (2000) *Ulice moga grada: antropologija domaćeg terena* (Belgrade: Biblioteka XX vek).

Russell, P. A. (1997) Musical tastes and society, in: D. J. Hargreaves & A. C. North (Eds), *The Social Psychology of Music* (Oxford: Oxford University Press).

Šarac, D. & Jelaca, M. (2001) Povratak gladiatora, *Slobodna Dalmacija*, 18 June.

Šćepanović, I. (2003) Neće biti incidenata jer ja odašiljem pozitivnu energiju, *Slobodna Dalmacija*, 3 December.

Senjković, R. (2002) *Lica društva, likovi države* (Zagreb: Biblioteka Nova etnologija).

Senjković, R. & Dukić, D. (2005) Virtual homeland? Reading the music on offer on a particular web page, *International Journal of Cultural Studies*, 8(1), pp. 44–62.

Stanić, R. (2002) Balašević: Umalo da postanem muška Brena, *Blic News*, 20 November.

Stanivuković, Z. (2002) Naličje "istočnog greha", *NIN*, 25 April.

Stojčić, D. (2002) Kolobarić: može nastupiti u Osijeku, ali ne i u HNK-u, *Glas Slavonije*, 7 May.

Strukar, V. (2003a) Grčki Telecom s 250 tisuća dolara sponzorira moj spot za MTV, *Novi list*, 4 May.

Strukar, V. (2003b) Severina, Ceca i Lepa Brena zajedno pjevale u Sava centru!, *Novi list*, 13 March.

Strukar, V. (2004) Mikulić je dao sve od sebe, *Novi list*, 13 May.

Strukar, V. & Mamić, Z. (2003) Nikad mizernija kvaliteta pjesama, *Novi list*, 4 March.

Trajković, J. (2004) Srbi ugodno iznenadjeni, mnogi i šokirani, *Jutarnji list*, 17 May.

Turina, D. (2000) Dobro veče, Hrvatska, *Novi list*, 6 December.

Ugrešić, D. (1998) *The Culture of Lies: Anti-Political Essays* (London: Phoenix).

Velikonja, M. (2002) Ex-home: 'Balkan culture' in Slovenia after 1991, in: S. Resić & B. Tornquist Plewa (Eds), *The Balkans in Focus: Cultural Boundaries in Europe* (Lund: Nordic Academic Press).

Vertovec, S. (1999) Conceiving and researching transnationalism, *Ethnic and Racial Studies*, 22(2), pp. 447–462.

Vertovec, S. (2001) Transnationalism and identity, *Journal of Ethnic and Migration Studies*, 27(4), pp. 573–582.

Vodopija, Z. (2004) Hrvatski sluh za srpski folk, *Vjesnik*, 18 May.

Volčič, Z. (2005) Belgrade vs Serbia: spatial re-configurations of belonging, *Journal of Ethnic and Migration Studies*, 31(4), pp. 639–658.

Volčič, Z. (forthcoming) Spaces of identity and belonging: narratives of young Macedonian and Slovenian intellectuals, *Cultural Dynamics*.

Vuković, Ž. (1998) Rambove turbo-folk karikature, *Večernji list*, 12 December.

Zakošek, N. (2000) The legitimation of war: political construction of a new reality, in: N. Skopljanac Brunner *et al.* (Eds), *Media and War* (Zagreb: Centre for Transition and Civil Society Research and Belgrade: Agency Argument).

Žužić, B. (2002) Bajagin koncert u Labinu, *Slobodna Dalmacija*, 27 August.

Ten Years Later: The Changing Nature of Transnational Ties in Post-independence Croatia

DAPHNE WINLAND

Perhaps one of the most difficult test cases for political scientists and historians of the past 50 years has been the drama that began to unfold in Eastern Europe in 1989. Seemingly overnight, the region was thrust into a tumult at every level—political, economic, religious, cultural and familial. Few international political events captured the world's attention during the early 1990s as did the war in former Yugoslavia. By the late 1980s, and especially following the rise to power of the Yugoslav president Slobodan Milošević in 1987, signs of the tragedy that was to unfold became apparent. Apart from the looming political and economic crises facing Yugoslavia, the fragility of the state was evidenced in faltering support for the preservation of Yugoslav unity.

Throughout the decade these events played out in the mass media—in newspapers, and on the radio, television and the internet—often graphically highlighting the violence of the conflict while at the same time situating so-called 'ethnic' tensions at the centre of these struggles. The views and images that dominated media accounts of atrocities and incomprehensible destruction in former Yugoslavia, particularly in places like Croatia and Bosnia and Herzegovina, depicted a region condemned to endless cycles of violence because of "age old ethnic hatreds" (Kaplan, 1994). The power of the images of this war for the collective imagination made such explanations not only plausible but convincing. It was but one flawed perspective among many on the causes of the disintegration of Yugoslavia.

There is now little doubt about the global significance of the wars of Yugoslav succession of the 1990s, whatever their causes, as demonstrated by the many books and articles written on the subject. The literature on the region is replete with myriad debates on the issues of nationalism, the nation-state and its futures, ethnic conflict, civil society, and even the contemplation of apocalyptic themes of '*fin de siècle*' (Fukuyama, 1993) and 'the clash of civilizations' (Huntington, 1993; 1996). Such titles as *Balkan Tragedy* (Woodward, 1995), *Balkan Babel* (Ramet, 1996), *The Tragedy of Yugoslavia* (Seroka and Pavlović 1992), *Broken Bonds* (Cohen, 1993), *Balkan Ghosts* (Kaplan, 1994), *The Death of Yugoslavia* (Silber and Little, 1995) and *The Destruction of Yugoslavia* (Magaš, 1993) betray not only a general lack of consensus on the causes of the wars, but the tenor of shock and dismay.[1]

Many were caught off guard by the events leading up to this period, precipitating questions concerning the nature and rise of ethnic nationalism but, more generally, on the relevance or viability of modernist perspectives on the future of nationalism. Scholars, political leaders and policy makers were scrambling to make sense of the eruption of violence and nationalist fervour in Yugoslavia and fretting over the implications of the conflict for the European Union, pluralism and a democratic future for the region. Among the explanations proposed by those interested or anxious to understand the conflicts in former Yugoslavia were external precipitants (for example, premature recognition of Slovenia and Croatia) and internal factors (often in the form of theories of national character, 'ancient ethnic hatreds', historical and/or systemic factors) (cf. Ramet, 2004). For example, a central theme or lens through which these conflicts were popularly viewed was that we were merely witnessing the spectacular re-emergence of long suppressed ethnic hatreds (Kaplan, 1994; Fukuyama, 1994). That is, within former Yugoslavia, communities were historically organized along discrete and bounded ethnic lines, and that the unravelling of Yugoslavia merely allowed for these distinct and conflicting ethnic identities to coalesce into new nation-states. This controversial, mostly discredited perspective found proponents both in and outside former Yugoslavia.

For those who favour perspectives based on systemic economic and political variables there is compelling evidence that points to the importance of global economic forces in hastening the process of Yugoslavia's disintegration. The drastic decline in living standards and austerity measures, brought on by international pressure to resolve its foreign debt crisis in the 1980s, contributed greatly to the disintegration of government authority and its ability to perform its function of preserving local political and civil order (Woodward, 1995). The difficulties in rapidly transforming a socialist state into a democratic market economy (a transition demanded by foreign creditors and Western governments) thus exacerbated the region's vulnerability—one based on decades of dependence on Western powers (Offe, 1997).[2] Competition and conflict between leaders of the republics, particularly over their commitments to the terms of the debt repayment package in an already highly decentralized Yugoslav federation, further set the stage for the collapse of the social order. The very foundation of communities, namely the protections and rights guaranteed under the state system, were seriously compromised.

This sampling of macro-political and economic explanations provides a broader context within which to understand the tragic fate of Yugoslavia. What becomes clear, however, in analysing the causes and consequences of the dissolution of the federation is that insufficient attention has been paid to the processes, both locally and globally inflected, associated with transnationalism, specifically the roles and relationships of Yugoslav citizens at home and abroad. Other than agonizing over the causes of the unthinkable brutality between neighbours (i.e. via explanations that hinge on 'national character' and 'cultures of violence'), there has been little attention paid to how, for example, Serbs and Croats abroad were implicated in the Yugoslav wars of succession. These diasporas were instrumental in shaping Yugoslav politics before, during and after the war.

Where it has been discussed, transnationalism has been heralded as a force for political, economic and social integration into Europe. Thus transnationalism has great appeal for those in Eastern Europe concerned with EU enlargement. Among other things, it is also seen to represent a potentially liberalizing and unifying force, specifically through the transnational transmission of liberal–democratic values, a view which shares common ground with proponents of civil society and liberalism. The political theorist Will Kymlicka, ever the optimist, has argued that liberalism, in its particularistic historical and indigenous forms, has a long legacy in Eastern Europe (Kymlicka, 2001). But this legacy has been overshadowed by centuries of imperial rule and the recent experience of communism. Therefore he argues that Western models for the accommodation of minority differences will appeal to Eastern Europeans and can be relevant for the region, particularly through the importation of liberal pluralist political culture from the West. This view, however, oversimplifies the diverse histories and peoples of the region, the complex realities of societal change and, more importantly, the role of transnationalism in this process, namely the *negotiation of* and *contestation over* rather than the *transmission of* ('Western') values and principles by those affected by them.

Of particular interest here is the impact of transnationalism, specifically diaspora involvement in the events following the break-up of former Yugoslavia and the emergence of Croatia as a nation-state. The particular challenges of Croatia and Croats are unique, important and instructive in discussions of transnationalism and its implications for thinking about the Balkans. The story of Croatia's eventual independence from Yugoslavia began in much the same way as that of most of the states that emerged after the Cold War in Europe ended in 1989. The threat of a Croatian multiparty democratic system to Slobodan Milošević's hold on the federal Yugoslav state led to the rapid deterioration of relations with the Croatian republic. Milošević's truculence proved decisive in Croatia's decision to pursue the path of independence rather than opt for the earlier Croatian offer of a compromise giving Croatia more autonomy under Yugoslav rule. The war which erupted shortly after caused untold damage, the human costs of which are inestimable (Thomas, 1999; Glenny, 1992, 1999).

However, Croatia has received proportionately less attention than other successor states. While most media and scholarly attention has focused on the heinous crimes orchestrated by Slobodan Milošević in Bosnia and Herzegovina and Croatia, thanks to its unique history and positioning in Yugoslavia and its particularly brutal war experience, Bosnia has received the lion's share of attention. Serbia and Kosovo also received a great deal of coverage, particularly towards the end of the 1990s. At the beginning of the war in

Croatia in 1991 Croatians were seen as not much more than victims of Serb aggression and, later, as perpetrators of the same in Serb enclaves of Croatia, such as Krajina, and in Bosnia and western Hercegovina.

In the midst of the convulsive changes brought about by war and independence in Croatia, Croatians were trying to (re)create a new/old state. With the erosion of Yugoslav state institutions and the lack of independent ones to take their place, steps were taken in Croatia to found independent political parties in 1990,[3] all of which sought in different ways to deal with the Croatian national question. The Croatian experience has been strongly influenced by transnational processes at every level—political, economic and social. The experience of war and independence in Croatia precipitated changes for Croats both within and outside the new state. Thus, in cities such as Melbourne, Chicago, Washington and Toronto, one could not help but notice an endless number of protests and demonstrations by diaspora communities actively engaged in supporting the process of Croatian national reconfiguration. The transnational resources which were tapped by the new Croatian state significantly affected and continue to influence the course of politics in Croatia.

Much scholarly discussion has focused on the role of transnationalism primarily from the perspective of diasporas as purveyors of, on the one hand, values, ideals and identifications and, on the other, as providers of political resources and economic involvement in homeland affairs. As transnational actors, diaspora Croats have been exemplars of the intersections between the social, cultural, economic and political dimensions of the 'transition' in the Balkans. They have been implicated in the post-war political transition by the Tudjman government in their appointed roles as ministers and as beneficiaries of choice business and investment opportunities. Diaspora Croats see their often self-appointed role as custodians of key Croatian cultural values, memories and heritage essential to the preservation of Croatian national identity. In diaspora interactions with the homeland one sees both the continuities and the tensions involved in negotiating a contemporary, relevant and meaningful space, both at home and abroad. Diaspora–homeland relations thus provide an interesting prism through which to examine the possibilities and limitations of transnationalism as a concept, a set of relationships and a set of practices.

I therefore investigate the role of transnationalism in the production of meaning around the formation of a Croatian national identity and the struggle to shed unwanted images and introduce a renewed Croatia/n to the world. To this end, I discuss diaspora political involvement in homeland affairs as well as their familial, affective and informal relations with homeland Croatians. Although less visible than those involving international relations, trade and diplomacy, these are ubiquitous in so far as transnational relations are concerned. Aside from the highly visible role of diaspora Croats during the lead-up to the war and independence, the diaspora has played a mostly informal, though critical, role in the homeland. This has specifically involved sending remittances to family in the homeland, organizing relief and fundraising drives, lobbying host governments for international recognition, sponsoring family to emigrate, and initiating, disrupting and/or maintaining connections that define Croatians to each other and to the world.

Diaspora Croat Involvements in the New Homeland

The role of the diaspora in Croatian homeland affairs is not only a product of independence in 1991. The political engagement of diaspora Croats with the homeland began in earnest at the end of the 19th and beginning of the 20th centuries in North America with large scale emigration from Croatia and the need to maintain ties with family back home. Early on the emergence of homeland-focused diaspora Croat organizations was a direct response to political turmoil in what was to become Yugoslavia. For example, the centralization efforts of the Hungarian monarchy in the late 19th century resulted in political divisions between Croats (specifically loyalists and those who favoured Croatian independence) and accelerated diaspora political action aimed at securing a Croatian homeland. Throughout the 20th century, diaspora Croats have been variously involved with the homeland, ranging from the sending of remittances to the activities of small, but vocal, radical extremist movements aimed at bringing down Tito's regime. The spectre of Croatian independence, however, raised the political ante for diaspora Croats globally.

While some scholars have mentioned the more recent role of the diaspora in the first Croatian president Franjo Tudjman's ascent to power in 1990 (Pusić, 1995; 1997a; 1997b; Tanner, 1996; Goldstein, 1999), only the political analyst Paul Hockenos (2003) has gone beyond a brief, albeit journalistic, description of the political and financial influence of specifically right-wing diaspora Croats during and immediately following war and independence.[4] Diaspora Croats, who are vocal and feel they have a stake—economic, political and/or emotional—in Croatia, often join forces with nationalist parties and interests. Among many other things, diaspora Croats in general have been referred to as the 'third pillar of the Croatian national budget'. They have played a central role in the conservative politics of the homeland. While this is not unusual as far as diaspora political involvements go,[5] the diaspora Croat case is more complex than that usually conveyed by scholars or analysts of diaspora politics, which suggests that they have had a singularly negative political effect on homeland politics.

These and other dimensions of the transnational relations that characterize diaspora Croats and the homeland do not conform to the expectations of many theorists, specifically those who speak enthusiastically of the potential of transnational identifications to transcend modernist constructs and statist categories. For example, the 'betweenness' that is celebrated by many theorists (Bhabha, 1990; Appadurai, 1996) as a diaspora's 'empowering paradox', it is argued, unmoors the congruence of territory and culture central to nationalist claims (Miyoshi & Harootunian, 1993; Jusdanis, 2001). In effect, the often nationalist activities and narratives that diasporas frequently espouse and promote have actually served to reinforce a modernist conception of the nation-state, albeit through transnational means.

Diaspora Croats have been implicated in the state-building (*državotvorna*) programme since before independence was declared in 1990. Many have enthusiastically embraced the efforts of Croatian politicians to involve them in Croatian national affairs. Through fund-raising and lobbying, volunteering for both the military and rebuilding efforts, Croatian social and symbolic sensibilities about themselves as a nation and as a people were reinvigorated by independence. In this context absolutist notions of Croatian origin, territoriality and belonging were consistently reinforced by those on the right of the political spectrum in Croatia and in the diaspora. For example, although a law of return for diaspora was never formally implemented, key sections of Croatian constitutional laws on citizenship are devoted to diaspora returnees. Article 16 of the 1991 Law on Citizenship of the Croatian constitution guarantees automatic citizenship to anyone who "issues a written statement that he or she considers himself or herself to be a Croatian citizen" (Croatian Constitution, 1991). Among the measures that Tudjman undertook after he came to power in 1990 was the creation of special government offices and of the Ministry of Return and Immigration (Ministarstva Povratka i Useljeništva) to represent the Croatian population abroad.[6] During the 1990s the ministry adjusted its mandate several times to reflect the changing priorities of the state. For example, the Ministry of Return and Immigration became the Ministry for Development, Emigration and Reconstruction.

While diaspora Croats were actively pursued by the first Croatian government of Franjo Tudjman, the left-of-centre coalition government of 2000–03 was not as supportive of diaspora returnees. Eventually the ministry was absorbed into the Croatian Foreign Ministry to become the Office for Croatian Minorities, Emigration and Immigration. According to a Croatian government press release circulated in 2000:

> There will no longer be a specialised administration or department dealing only in issues relating to emigrants or returnees. During recent changes to the organisation of state bodies, the new government did not adopt the proposal of the Sabor [Parliament] Committee for Emigration that business relating to emigrants and returnees be taken over by the Ministry for Reconstruction, Construction and Public Enterprise. The Committee believes that a special administration in the above ministry would be more appropriate as experience in the field shows that emigrants and returnees encounter the most problems in those areas. . .As a special ministry or department no longer exists, returnees and emigrants will have to adapt to the new system. . .We hope that these will be more understanding and helpful and that the procedure is simpler.

As expected, many diaspora Croats were furious over the implementation of these measures and voiced their concerns through the Croatian World Congress and other diaspora organizations, as well as to the Croatian government itself. They felt that this particular change was symptomatic of what they claimed was the increasingly hostile attitude of the coalition government towards the diaspora in general. Many felt that they were being punished because the diaspora overwhelmingly (63%) supported the Croatian Democratic Community (HDZ) in the 2000 elections. All six members elected by the diaspora were HDZ.

Since the January 2000 elections, the influence of the Croatian diaspora on homeland political and economic affairs has diminished considerably, demonstrating the recognition by Croatian leaders of the political influence of diaspora Croats. Measures have included the closure of the former Ministry of Return and Immigration, delays in the tabling of a Bill of Returnees modelled on the Israeli 'Law of Return', the closing of some consular offices in the USA and Australia, and the parliamentary review of the 'special diaspora ticket' (which reserved 12 seats in the Croatian parliament for diaspora representatives), introduced by HDZ into the Croatian constitution in 1995. The perceived need of the then ruling coalition to distance itself from the legacy of the HDZ was expedited in part through the marginalization of diaspora Croats, most of whom directly or indirectly supported the HDZ. The controversial removal in 2000 of Ante Beljo (a prominent returnee from Canada and past member of Otpor (a radical right-wing diaspora organization) and now the director of the Croatian Information Centre in Zagreb), then executive director of the Croatian state-supported diaspora organization, the Croatian Homeland Foundation (HMI), illustrates the implications of these changes for diaspora

Croats. His removal enraged members of the Croatian World Congress, a broad-based diaspora organization.

Since the heady days of the early 1990s diaspora Croats have been variously attuned to homeland affairs and have more or less adjusted to the reality of an independent Croatia. While diaspora–homeland networks fostered through the church, family and community continue to be relevant, attitudes to Croatia have changed somewhat since Tudjman's time. Although many diaspora Croats feel they have been virtually eliminated from state decision-making structures and direct involvement in homeland politics, there are many who state that, so long as they can continue to recast and/or maintain their involvement and connections to the homeland through, for example, visits to Croatia, they are satisfied.

There are those, of course, who work tenaciously to remain involved in a variety of capacities. Most recently diaspora Croats have been at the forefront of efforts to exonerate General Ante Gotovina. Since his International Criminal Tribunal for Yugoslavia (ICTY) indictment, Ante Gotovina has become a national hero not only to many Croats but also to diaspora Croats. Many articles and testimonials have been written extolling his credentials as a Croatian patriot and much of his support comes from diaspora Croats. For example, the website devoted to him (http://www.AnteGotovina.com) is sponsored by the Croatian American Association.

Regardless of how well informed or interested they are in contemporary Croatian homeland affairs, most diaspora Croats continue to have strong opinions about the new homeland and, most significantly, their relationship to it now that Croatia is independent. Criticism of the communist-era Yugoslav political system has been a diaspora pastime for decades, as has criticism of the nature and pace of the 'transition' from communism since 1990. The concern with democratic political values and the diaspora's role as purveyor of these values is revealed in its opinions and actions. Typical comments from diaspora Croats include: "People I know back home are used to having had everything done for them under the communists. Now they constantly complain that things aren't what they expected. They're lazy, to tell you the truth", or "The mentality of Croatians back home is stuck in old Yugoslavia".

While diaspora Croats generally argue that Croatians in the new state should be left to chart their own course, there are those who have felt that homeland Croatians should look to *them* for inspiration and guidance in their 'transition to democracy', i.e. for the transmission of democratic values and principles and practices. As one observed: "Croatians at home don't know the meaning of democracy. They have been under the Communists for so long. They have a lot to learn." Clearly homeland Croatians do not live up to the nostalgic imaginings or expectations of the diaspora. There are always those diaspora Croats who, whatever their motivations, persist in providing mostly unsolicited 'expert advice' to homeland Croatian authorities, family and friends and in otherwise attempting to insert themselves into Croatian homeland affairs. They are confident in their assessments of life in Croatia and, more importantly, of what Croatia and Croatians need. Reception of these overtures by homeland Croatians is invariably and increasingly chilly.

Although diaspora Croats have less political clout than they used to, their presence is still felt. The re-election of the HDZ in November 2003 was seen as a positive change by many in the diaspora who felt that HDZ was the only party that shared their vision for the homeland and valued their input. Boris Mikšić, a Croatian American businessman from Minnesota (and a hard-line nationalist, named Croatia's honorary consul in

Minnesota by Tudjman) made a bid for the Croatian presidency in late 2004. He worked hard at courting the diaspora vote in Germany, Minnesota, Washington, Chicago, Los Angeles and Toronto. In October 2004, however, he announced that he was withdrawing his candidacy because he felt that the Croatian (homeland) media was boycotting him. He subsequently decided to run as an independent presidential candidate. While he finished third in the ballot, garnering 17.8% of votes, he contested the results, saying that he should have had a place in the run-off between the first placed incumbent Stipe Mesić and second placed Jadranka Kosor, a Croatian cabinet minister. He alleged that the elections were rigged—a claim rejected by the state-run Croatian Electoral Commission and by non-governmental observers. Recently Mikšić has stated that he plans to form a political party and compete in Zagreb's mayoral race in 2005. Mikšić is by no means a benign presence in Croatia. Currently Ivo Sanader, whose political fortunes are waning, sees Mikšić as a political liability in his relations with the EU, given Mikšić's right-wing politics and generally sceptical views on EU membership. The challenge posed by this diaspora Croat is indicative of the degree to which such people remain a potentially significant cause for concern.

Croatians at 'Home'

Any discussion of transnationalism and diaspora must take into account the homeland, and not just its political and economic characteristics, but its people. The centrality of homeland Croatians to the views, connections and formation of diaspora Croat identifications, past and present, is crucial to a comprehensive analysis of transnational relations in the Croatian context. The response of homeland Croatians in particular to diaspora involvement in Croatian affairs has ranged from ambivalent to negative. For their part, homeland Croatians have by and large rejected and/or resisted diaspora efforts to assume a role in the development of a vision for the new Croatia/n. While diaspora Croats have been variously concerned and involved, either in spirit or in practice, in Croatian independence, they have also been the collective 'whipping boy' for homeland Croatians. This can be attributed to a number of factors, some of which implicate diaspora Croats directly and others of which reflect general discouragement over the nature and pace of change in Croatia.

Since independence, homeland Croatians have encountered the best and the worst that the West has to offer and have consequently had to re-evaluate their lives, ambitions and goals in light of these changes. Over the course of my research in Croatia (1997–present), many have felt that the main beneficiaries of independence and all that has come in its wake have been those well placed to take advantage of political contacts and opportunities afforded to the financially and politically well connected. While doing research in Croatia, I found that the term 'diaspora' was also one that aroused sentiments of ambivalence, antagonism or derision. It did not seem to matter who I was speaking to: mention of diaspora Croats regularly elicited negative comments. What comes through in homeland Croats' responses is resentment and/or ambivalence toward the diaspora for a variety of reasons. These include what is viewed as the retention of a vulgarized ethnic culture and obsolete political ideals; capitalizing on investment opportunities of questionable benefit to homeland Croatians; and meddling in Croatian internal political affairs. Homeland Croats' impressions and expectations of diaspora Croats (e.g. diaspora privilege, materialism, ignorance of homeland issues) have had a strong impact on diaspora–homeland relations, regardless of the personal connections (family, friends) they maintain with diaspora Croats.

Although the homeland Croatians interviewed over the course of my research admired, sometimes grudgingly, the financial success of diaspora Croats, they had little that was positive to say about their 'Croatness'. Rather, they found their cultural idioms, references and practices outmoded. The mainly ethno-cultural emphasis of diaspora Croat nationalism is not easily compatible with that which operates in the Croatian social and political realm. For example, my questions concerning the involvement of the diaspora in Croatian politics were often greeted with scowls. Others criticized the often right-wing nationalistic views of diaspora Croats as anachronistic, jingoistic, out of step with current realities in Croatia and damaging to its image abroad. "They are a bunch of romantic idealists living in the past" (house renovator, Zagreb, October 2000). "They are nationalists from the last century" (NGO worker, Zagreb, November 2002). Many also condemned the diaspora Croat from Hercegovina, Gojko Šušak. Šušak, Croatia's ultra-nationalist defence minister (until his death in 1998) hailed from Ottawa, Canada. The popular Croatian satirical writer and journalist Tanja Torbarina dubbed him "pizza man" in her column in 1995 in the Croatian weekly *Globus*, and the name stuck. In their eyes Šušak epitomized what is wrong with the relationship between Croatia and the diaspora. He was often criticized for financing and essentially running the Croat region of Bosnia and Hercegovina, profiteering from black-market arms dealing, subverting the Dayton Peace Accords and hiding indicted war criminals. Ironically, then, while Croatian political leaders and elites (specifically those associated with the HDZ) endlessly praised and commended the contributions and commitment of the diaspora and of Bosnian Croats to Croatia's freedom and prosperity (not to mention making frequent references to their presumed ethnic 'purity'), Croatians in the homeland often regarded them with disdain.

Many comments reflected sentiments ranging from ambivalence to outright scorn: "I don't understand why they feel they have a right to say anything about what goes on here!" (retired female factory worker, Zagreb, November 2003). Most also expressed resentment at what they argued was not only the often preachy and, some say, generally superior attitude of diaspora Croats towards them, but also at the high regard with which they have been held by Croatian politicians (from the HDZ in particular and from other right-of-centre parties). Before the change of government in January 2000 Croatians frequently remarked negatively on comments made by public officials and politicians praising the contributions of diaspora Croats to Croatia's fight for independence and their contributions to the homeland. They further expressed frustration with the view held by some prominent Croatians that they—the homeland lot—were somehow suspect for having remained in Croatia. They were seen as either 'stupid' for not taking advantage of economic opportunities outside Croatia or somehow lacking initiative and Croatian political or national consciousness, "as if nothing has happened to us in Croatia over the past 50, never mind the past six years!"(high school teacher, Zagreb, April 1997). The implication of this view for some was that many homeland Croatians tacitly accepted Tito's communist regime and/or that they were ignorant. Some also commented on the irony of the frequent depiction of diaspora Croats by HDZ officials as 'political' émigrés—suggesting that those who left the homeland did so because they were denied employment or faced other forms of persecution in Yugoslavia because of their nationalist or political views. The underlying reasons for these attitudes toward the Croatian diaspora reflect concerns, some of which are quite common among homeland peoples, such as what is viewed as the retention of romantic and anachronistic views, and an inordinate amount of influence in Croatian political and financial sectors.

Attention to homeland attitudes towards diaspora ways of being Croatian are as important as are political differences of opinion. Although, generally speaking, Western social, cultural and political influences are valorized by many homeland Croatians, they do *not* look to diaspora Croats living in the West as a source of inspiration or advice. The almost unanimously negative opinions voiced by many speak to a general desire to embrace change, shed their Balkan image and promote a distinctively modern European politics and persona. Thus, diaspora Croats, often represented as unsophisticated, provide a critical reference point for those homeland Croatians who are eager to distance themselves from their collective past (exemplified in the preoccupations of diaspora Croats with tradition) and to reinforce their image as modern Croatians/Europeans.

Conclusions

Post-communist societies are increasingly drawn into an ever-expanding and often perplexing array of networks and linkages, a fact that is recognized and addressed by scholars, but only partially. While a great deal of attention has focused on the impacts of globalization on the political and economic state of post-communist Europe, little of that attention has been directed at transnationalism and its complex role in producing distinctive social practices and differentiated identities. For Croats, these have been influenced by centuries of wars, invasions and empires, as well as by shifting borders and balances of power involving competing visions of peoplehood. This has included the imperial identifications of Austro-Hungarian, pan-Slavic unity and Yugoslavism in its various forms. This historical context, defined by social and political turmoil, has shaped the sensibilities with which Croatians have come to experience the contemporary reality of Croatian identity and statehood.

The promise of the new post-socialist Croatia in 1990 was one of purpose and pride, stability and certainty reflected in ubiquitous pronouncements on the strength and resilience of the Croatian national character. However, when the moment of possibility finally arrived in 1991, it did not produce the clarity of vision and purpose that had been the rallying cry for all Croats who had fought and/or waited for the day when Croatia would be free of communist rule. Soon after the initial euphoria of independence, the contradictions and complexity that characterize Croatia intensified.

The combined economic, political, symbolic and interpersonal changes in the Croatian context provide insights into the unique ways in which transnationalism reverberates through the quotidian realities of the post-communist transition. The value of the Croatian example is demonstrated by how transnational processes can be directly related to the experience of difference in homelands. Thus, rather than undermining the classic modernist logic of the nation-state (Clifford, 1994; Kaplan, 1996), diasporas can in fact reinforce it through support for (ethnically based) territorial claims in the homeland, notions of origin and true belonging.[7] In effect, the often nationalist activities and narratives that diaspora Croats frequently espouse and promote have actually served to reinforce a modernist conception of the new Croatia, albeit through transnational means. Thus the presumption that the dismantling of the communist-era state control creates the conditions for emancipation, through transnational linkages that will stimulate further European integration, is not grounded in sufficient empirical evidence. The events of the past decade demonstrate the emergence of numerous and often competing political and economic trends—liberal democratic, authoritarian and otherwise. There is room for cautious optimism, however, particularly if the national and the transnational are seen as processes through which Croatians can productively and creatively engage in reconfiguring Croatianess.

In Croatia multiple vectors of identification currently circulate, including liberalism, nationalism, European, cosmopolitanism, *Hrvatstvo* (Croatness) and ethnicity, all of which are shaped by historical, social and political forces, locally, regionally, nationally and transnationally. These suggest a process of negotiation and contestation rather than simply the transmission of values transnationally. As Massey *et al.*, have suggested, ethnic national sentiments, while prevalent in Croatia, have been increasingly coupled with views that are distinctly liberal. Their overall findings point to the fact that "the core of political liberalism...is widespread and may grow, not at the expense but alongside current nationalist sentiments" (2003, p. 76). So too perhaps for diaspora.

Notes

1. Scholarly perspectives on changes in former Yugoslavia since 1989 range from geopolitical and policy-oriented analyses to personal accounts and reflective essays. Many, however, also became caught up in conflictive narratives of responsibility (Kennedy, 2002; Wachtel, 1998), sometimes characterized by accusations of guilt and culpability, as is evidenced in the arguments and critiques of Cushman (1997), Denitch (1994), Meštrović (1996), Hayden (1992, 1996, 1997) and Magaš (1993).
2. For example, the end of the Cold War undermined Yugoslavia's strategic position (as a bulwark against the USSR). The two Yugoslavias (1918–41 and 1945–91) were both shaped by the postwar settlements of Western European powers.
3. For example, the right-wing Hrvatski oslobodilački pokret (HOP) and the Hrvatska stranka prava (HSP), as well as the centrist Hrvatska socijalno liberalna stranka (HSLS) and, later, the leftist Socijaldemokratska partija Hrvatske (SDP) were created around this time.
4. However, Hockenos's book on exile patriotism amongst Croats, Serbs and Albanians focuses exclusively on those right-wing Toronto Croats who catapulted Tudjman to power (Hockenos, 2003).
5. Cf. work on Israel and its Jewish diasporas (Sheffer, 1986; Shain, 2000).
6. The Ministry of Return and Immigration also published a magazine, called *Bilten*, chronicling government programmes and returnee experiences.
7. According to Greta Slobin (2001, p. 524), for example, in the Russian critic Chelyshev's assessment of Russian emigré literature, rather than preserving Russian humanist scholarship, the heterogeneity of the Russian diaspora comes through, reflecting, among other things, a neo-conservative nationalist agenda. Similarly, Raeff (1990) points to the (political) conservatism epitomized in the exiled writer Alexander Solzhenitsyn's critiques of Western values. Others have also emphasized the conservative/nationalist leanings of diaspora groups (e.g. Hindu diasporas, cf. Rai, 1995).

References

Appadurai, A. (1996) The production of locality, in: Appadurai, *Modernity at Large: Cultural Dimensions of Globalization*, pp. 78–200 (Minneapolis, MN: University of Minnesota Press).
Bhabha, H. (1990) The third space, in: J. Rutherford (Ed.), *Identity, Community, Culture, Difference*, pp. 207–221 (London: Lawrence and Wishart).
Clifford, J. (1994) Diasporas, *Cultural Anthropology*, 9(3), pp. 302–338.
Cohen, L. (1993) *Broken Bonds: Yugoslavia's Disintegration and Balkan Politics in Transition* (Oxford: Westview Press).
Croatian Constitution (1991) The Law on Croatian Citizenship, available online at: http://www.sabor.hr/sabor/parliament/acts/propis13.htm.

Cushman, T. (1997) Critical theory and the war in Croatia and Bosnia, *Donald W. Treadgold Papers in Russian, East European and Central Asian Studies*, 13, Henry M. Jackson School of International Studies, University of Washington.

Denitch, B. (1994) Dismembering Yugoslavia: nationalist ideologies and the symbolic revival of genocide, *American Ethnologist*, 21(3), pp. 367–390.

Fukuyama, F. (1994) The war of all against all, *New York Times Book Review*, 10 April, p. 7.

Fukuyama, F. (1993) *The End of History and the Last Man* (New York: Avon Books).

Glenny, M. (1992) *The Fall of Yugoslavia: The Third Balkan War* (London: Penguin).

Glenny, M. (1999) *The Balkans: Nationalism, War and the Great Powers, 1804–1999* (London: Granta Books).

Goldstein, I. (1999) *Croatia: A History*, trans. N. Jovanović (Montreal: McGill-Queens University Press).

Hayden, R. (1992) Constitutional nationalism in the formerly Yugoslav republics, *Slavic Review*, 51(4), pp. 654–673.

Hayden, R. (1996) Imagined communities and the real victim: self-determination and ethnic cleansing in Yugoslavia, *American Ethnologist*, 23(4), pp. 783–801.

Hayden, R. (1997) The tactical uses of passion, *Current Anthropology*, 38(5), pp. 924–925.

Hockenos, P. (2003) *Homeland Calling: Exile Patriotism and the Balkan Wars* (Ithaca, NY: Cornell University Press).

Huntington, S. (1993) The clash of civilizations, *Foreign Affairs*, 72(3), pp. 23–49.

Huntington, S. (1996) *The Clash of Civilizations and the Remaking of World Order* (New York: Simon & Schuster).

Jusdanis, G. (2001) *The Necessary Nation* (Princeton, NJ: Princeton University Press).

Kaplan, C. (1996) *Questions of Travel: Postmodern Discourses of Displacement* (Durham, NC: Duke University Press).

Kaplan, R. (1994) *Balkan Ghosts: A Journey Through History* (New York: Vintage Books).

Kennedy, M. (2002) *Cultural Formations of Post-communism: Emancipation, Transition, Nation and War* (Minneapolis, MN: University of Minnesota Press).

Kymlicka, W. (2001) Western Political Theory and Ethnic Relations in Eastern Europe, in W. Kymlicka & M. Opalski (Eds) *Can Liberal Pluralism be Exported? Western Political Theory and Ethnic Relations in Eastern Europe* (New York: Oxford University Press) pp. 13–105.

Magaš, B. (1993) *The Destruction of Yugoslavia: Tracking the Break-up 1980–92* (London: Verso).

Massey, G., Hodson, R. & Sekulić, D. (2003) Nationalism, liberalism and liberal nationalism in post-war Croatia, *Nations and Nationalism*, 9(1), pp. 55–82.

Meštrović, S. (1996) *Genocide after Emotion: The Postemotional Balkan War* (London: Routledge).

Miyoshi, M. & Harootunian, H. D. (Eds) (1993) *Japan in the World* (Durham, NC: Duke University Press).

Offe, C. (1997) *Varieties of Transition: The East European and East German Experience* (Cambridge, MA: MIT Press).

Pusić, V. (1995) Uses of nationalism and the politics of recognition, *Anthropological Journal on European Cultures*, 4(1), pp. 43–61.

Pusić, V. (1997a) Croatia's struggle for democracy, *Revija za Sociologiju*, 28(2), pp. 95–110.

Pusić, V. (1997b) Croatia at the crossroads, paper presented at the International Forum for Democratic Studies of the National Endowment for Democracy, Washington, DC, 24 March.

Raeff, M. (1990) *Russia Abroad: A Cultural History of the Russian Emigration 1919–1939* (New York: Oxford University Press).

Rai, A. (1995) India on-line: electronic bulletin boards and the construction of a diasporic Hindu identity, *Diaspora*, 4(1), pp. 31–58.

Ramet, S. (1996) *Balkan Babel: The Disintegration of Yugoslavia from the Death of Tito to the Ethnic War* (Boulder, CO: Westview Press).

Ramet, S. (2004) "For a charm of pow'rful trouble, like a hell-broth boil and bubble": theories about the roots of the Yugoslav troubles, *Nationalities Papers*, 32(4), pp. 731–763.

Seroka, J. & Pavlović, V. (Eds) (1992) *The Tragedy of Yugoslavia: The Failure of Democratic Transformation* (Armonk, NY: M.E. Sharpe).

Shain, Y. (2000) American Jews and the construction of Israel's Jewish identity, *Diaspora*, 9(2), pp. 163–202.

Sheffer, G. (Ed.) (1986) *Modern Diasporas in International Politics* (London: Croom Helm).

Shukla, S. (1997) Building diaspora and nation: the 1991 'Cultural Festival of India', *Cultural Studies*, 11(3), pp. 296–315.

Slobin, G. (2001) The homecoming of the first wave diaspora and its legacy, *Slavic Review*, 60(3), pp. 513–529.

Silber, L. & Little, A. (1995) *The Death of Yugoslavia* (London: Penguin).

Tanner, M. (1996) *Croatia: A Nation Forged in War* (New Haven, CT: Yale University Press).

Thomas, R. (1999) *The Politics of Serbia in the 1990s* (New York: Columbia University Press).

Wachtel, A. (1998) *Making a Nation, Breaking a Nation: Literature and Cultural Politics in Yugoslavia* (Stanford, CA: Stanford University Press).

Woodward, S. L. (1995) *Balkan Tragedy: Chaos and Dissolution after the Cold War* (Washington, DC: Brookings Institution).

'Friends, Balkans, Statesmen Lend Us Your Ears': The Trans-state and State in Links between Turkey and the Balkans

ESRA BULUT

Policy makers have often cited 'human ties' as a factor in Turkish–Balkan interstate relations, mainly a reference to the sizeable number of people in Turkey of Balkan origin, and to perceived ethno-religious kin in the Balkans. Indeed, especially the latter have been key, at times critical, to inter-state relations. Rather than merely passive actors in the region's patterns of migration or processes of national integration, or solely sources of friction or collaberation in inter-state relations, members of these populations have themselves generated diverse links across borders. This paper examines the period since 1989, during which these populations have increasingly become subjects in relations between Turkey and the rest of the Balkans. Yet, precisely as trans-state ties have increased in significance, the 'state' has attempted to harness or infiltrate the 'trans-state' to further state interests. The paper seeks to show how non-state and state actors have interacted, resulting in an intensification and multiplication of trans-state ties. The focus is on the activities and politics surrounding the relevant populations in, and immigrants from, the former Yugoslav states, but this is placed within the wider regional context, including relevant populations in and from Bulgaria and Greece.

The paper is divided into two sections. In the first section the actors and processes that characterize trans-state ties are presented. I first discuss the non-state actors most relevant to the discussion, while showing the ways in which existing and new concepts are useful in understanding them. I then chart how, through trans-state ties, individuals and groups have adapted to, but also fed, the changing political, social, security and economic regional environment. In the second part of the article I show how popular assumptions about trans-states relations have to be discarded to correctly assess the nature and implications of the Turkish state's stance towards these ties. Three ways in which the state is present in the trans-state sphere are outlined in more detail. I conclude by relating these specific dynamics to broader trends of transnationalization and Europeanization in the Balkans. The findings of this paper caution against assumptions that either trend necessarily implies the decline of the nation-state.[1] The paper supports the position that further attention to the interaction between the trans-state and state holds the key to understanding how the peoples and polities of the Balkans relate to each other, to the rest of Europe and to the wider world.

Before proceeding, preliminary limitation and definition is necessary. For a working definition of transnational relations, I refer to Keohane and Nye who define them as "contracts, coalitions, and interactions across state boundaries that are not controlled by the central foreign policy organs of government" (1971, p. xi). As the conceived boundaries at stake are states, rather than nations, the term transnational is somewhat of a misnomer.[2] While the tendency in International Relations (IR) to equate nation with state has been widely discredited in recent years, terminological laziness and haziness still exists with regard to transnational relations. For reasons of clarity and consistency I will use the term 'trans-state' except where the term 'transnational' has been used by authors cited.

Envisaging Trans-state Actors

In this section, the groups and individuals involved and the terms commonly used in this context are examined. Ways to move with and beyond the terms and concepts to better capture the essence of developments are also suggested. For reasons of space, two types of group are focused on here: kin, on the one hand, and immigrants and diasporic communities, on the other.[3]

Who Constitutes Kin?

The term 'kin' has been used to describe the populations in the region with whom Turkey is envisaged to have a special relationship. In Turkish political discourse these references are common. In official references the Turkish Foreign Ministry has increasingly come to couple together the terms *Türk* and *akraba topluluklar* (related/family groups) when making official references to various groups in the region. The Diyanet İşleri Başkanlığı (DİB, State Religious Directorate) and the Diyanet Vakfı (DV, Religious Foundation) continue to refer to *soydaş ve dindaş* (co-ethnies and co-religionists). Interpreted in the widest sense, Muslim and/or Turkish-speaking populations in Bosnia-Herzegovina, Serbia and Montenegro (including Sandžak and Kosovo), Macedonia, Romania, Bulgaria, Albania and Greece all to varying degrees constitute potential, perceived, contested 'kin' for Turkey (Poulton & Taji-Farouki, 1997; Poulton, 1997a, 1997b).

However, the criteria for, or rationale behind envisaging, 'kin' is far from straightforward. This is partly because, as Hugh Poulton has highlighted, the question of who is a Turk in the Balkans has historically been an ambiguous and contested issue

(1997a). It is clear that defining kin as ethnic Turks is inadequate given the inclusion in the above of non-ethnic Turks and, depending on the population or area, various degrees of ambiguity between Turkish and Muslim identification. Equating kin with the broader category of Islamic practice or identification is also problematic.[4] While the two might be reasoned as roughly corresponding, any straightforward equation would obscure the complex interplay, overlap and distinctions between Ottoman legacy and tradition, Islamic practice and identification, and Turkish culture and identity in the region. Religious practice or identification is clearly not the sole factor in play, given ambiguities and distinctions between culture, historical legacy, faith, national identity and any affiliation with a particular state actor.

The 'Kin' is also a fluid concept over space and time—across countries and dependent partly on changing political and social conditions. Variations in census data regarding ethnic or national identification over time are just one of the more tangible ways in which this kind of fluidity can be detected. It follows that kin should not be understood as denoting a set of static and clearly definable groups, but as dependent on a variety of factors, in particular changing self-perceptions and the perceptions of others, especially in relation to the dominant ethnic group or the state. Another variable is the changing perception of potential kin groups regarding Turkey as a possible protector, ally or place of refuge, perhaps most striking in the case of the difference in the expectations and reality of life in Turkey for refugees who settled there during the exodus from Bulgaria in 1989 (Kumbetoglu, 1997; Nichols *et al.*, 2003). The 1990s conflicts also served as reminders that being associated with the Ottomans, or today with Turkey, has also constituted a liability for groups and individuals.[5]

In Turkey in the early and mid-1990s there was striking ignorance among the general public and political actors towards the Balkan region, coupled with a distorting Turkicizing of the Ottoman era. While extreme pan-Turkists promoted theories that Bosnian Muslims were really Turks, the nationalist–conservative intelligentsia displayed culturally based ethno-centrism, viewing the Ottoman experience from a retrospective nationalist perspective and presenting Muslims as having been part of the ruling nation (Bora, 1995, p. 278). After more than a decade during which the Turkish political elite and public have been exposed to information about the Balkans, perceptions are still very much shaped by ideological outlooks and identity-based assumptions about connections with the Balkans. In sum, far from being clear what kin is, the inter-state and trans-state interactions, some of which are outlined below, partly shape and determine who, and in what ways, constitute kin.

Immigrants, Diasporas?

Altogether several million Balkan immigrants and their descendents reside in Turkey today. One source puts the number of immigrants between 1923 and 1995 from the Balkans to Turkey at 1 643 058 (Greece: 424 625, Bulgaria: 790 717, Yugoslavia: 305 158 and Romania: 122 558), constituting most of the inward migration in those years (1 650 699).[6] This can be placed within a much longer period of migration as the Ottoman empire withdrew and almost continuous war conditions led to the mass migration of populations associated with Ottoman rule (Karpat, 2002). This long and varied history of migration stretching over the past two centuries necessitates wider terminology than the term 'immigrant' allows, given several generations who identify to varying degrees with the Balkans as place of origin, with the process of migration from the Balkans, or with more specific identities originating in the Balkans. This is evident from the various terms in Turkey used to describe these individuals and groups. While the terms *muhacir* (refugee) and *göçmen* (immigrant) are used quite widely and are not exclusive to the Balkans,[7] the terms *Balkan kökenli* (of Balkan origins/roots), *rumelili* (a person of Rumeli) and *mübadil* (exchangee of the 1923 official population exchange between Greece and Turkey) are also used. More specific terms are also employed relating to ethnicity, such as *Arnavut* (Albanian) and *Boşnak* (Bosniak); to town or area of origin such as *Prizrenli* (of Prizren), *Üsküplü* (of Skopje), *Giritli* (of Crete); to both references in the case of *Batı Trakya Türkleri* (West Thracian Turks) and *Rumeli Türkleri* (Turks of Rumeli); and to country of origin in the case of *Bulgaristan göçmeni* (immigrant from Bulgaria).

To dwell on the importance of naming, in the case of *Rumelili*, often used instead of immigrant or refugee, the distinctions between immigrant and non-immigrant are broken down—either deliberately or not—as Turkey partly lies in Rumeli, and the term carries connotations of a historical Ottoman region which transcended the national territories and borders which replaced it. Historically *Rumelili* constituted a key part of the nation-building elite, most notably in Mustafa Kemal Ataturk's personification of the nation in official Turkish nationalism, problematizing any notion of Balkan immigrants as existing on the margin of state or nation. Those with some Balkan connections are sometimes keen to emphasize this Rumeli identity, while some first generation immigrants are reluctant to use this term. In a very different way, the term *mübadil* has also come to signify identification with a particular historical process and can be seen as challenging the existing categories, and nationalizing and nation-state-centred narratives, in Turkey and Greece.[8]

All these names and emphases have been institutionalized in the civil society organizations and networks established in Turkey. All these usages hint at the multivaried possibilities of self- and other description and designation in which different reference points become less or more important as a result of historical, social and political factors. Thus I envisage all the terms outlined above as concepts to be analysed rather than clear analytical concepts—the term 'immigrant' is thus in this context used loosely in relation to a variety of groups who relate in various ways to the historical and ongoing processes of immigration from the rest of the Balkans to Turkey.

To varying degrees some populations within both kin and immigrant categories seem to fit the concept of an ethno-national diaspora, as defined as "a social-political formation, created as a result of either voluntary or forced migration, whose members regard themselves as of the same ethno-national origin and who permanently reside as minorities in one or several host countries" (Sheffer, 2003, pp. 9–10). According to Van Hear, who considers the Turks a diaspora in Bulgaria, and the events of 1989 as contributing to a partial de-diasporization, "the mass exodus of 1989 was congruent with the long-established flow of emigrants and the existing migration order—the in-gathering of the descendents of the Ottoman dispersal" (Van Hear, 1998, p. 216). Yet this is to take at face value the nationalist historiography of various Balkan states, including Turkey, and ignore the complex interplay of migration and conversion in the Islamicization and cultural Turkification of populations in the Balkans (Norris, 1993).[9] The constructedness of belonging, origins and homeland is exposed when we consider these groups comparatively. Are the Turks of Bulgaria a diaspora in Turkey or Bulgaria? If 'Rumeli Turks' are envisaged as having in fact 'returned' to Anatolia after diaspora existence in the Balkans, how can we make sense of many of the similarities in organization between these and some Bosnians and Albanians in Istanbul, seemingly constituting, or emerging as, diasporic communities in Turkey?

It seems that the traditional terms utilized have a number of shortcomings, supplying far too rigid or exclusive categories. The concept of 'diaspora space' may offer a partial solution to problems of envisaging the actors at play as the focus shifts from rigid categories of actors to diasporic processes. It is also useful in considering the question of 'homeland', problematized in the above examples, as it "includes the entanglement, the intertwining of the genealogies of dispersion with those of 'staying put'" (Brah, quoted in Jackson *et al.*, 2004, p. 3). Furthermore, it seems helpful to envisage the concept of homeland as an ambivalent and contested entity, and emphasize that 'going home' is not "necessarily desirable or natural" (Oxfeld & Long, 2004, p. 5), and that "a homeland has meaning even when people are ambivalent about it rather than identifying with a particular place" (Oxfeld & Long, 2004, p. 5). Immigrant association representatives in Turkey frequently refer to dual belonging, in keeping with diasporas around the world. An extreme manifestation of this can be seen in the words of Kenan Sahinler, President of Rumeli Turks Culture & Solidarity Association (RTKDD), claiming to speak on behalf of a series of Rumeli Associations and Foundations for the 650th anniversary of Turkish entry into the Balkans:

> As the Rumeli associations and foundations our aim is to be an example for the unity and integrity of Turkey by keeping our people forever unified and together. By means of the Celebration Week of the 650th Anniversary of Turks entering Rumeli, we once again remembered that Rumeli is a homeland we lost. But the territory of Turkey is our last motherland that will not be lost.[10]

Duality and ambivalence shape inter-state and trans-state politics. As Brubaker points out, "various homeland stances compete not only with one another but with stances that reject the basic premise of homeland politics ... The field of struggle to inflect state policy is therefore constituted by struggles over whether and how a state should be a homeland for its ethnic co-nationals in other states" (1996, p. 67). The concepts of 'diaspora' and 'homeland' are useful but should be referred to in full awareness of the ambiguity, and power of ambiguity, involved in their usage on the ground. If we are witnessing the formation or evolution of diasporic communities, the trans-state ties to which I now turn certainly influence their particular trajectories.

Increasing Trans-state Ties: Responses to, and Agents of, Change in the Region

This section outlines trans-state ties as a way in which individuals and groups have adapted, and further contributed, to their changing political, social, security and economic regional environment. As it would be beyond the scope of one paper to chart all changes in the region and attempt to relate them to trans-state ties, the implications of two broad categories of change in the political, social, security and economic environment will be explored in more detail here. The first covers the changes in communication and movement, making virtual and physical trans-state interaction between Turkey and the rest of the Balkans easier, quicker and more accessible. The second relates to the political changes, crises and conflicts that accompanied the demise of Yugoslavia and the emergence of successor states. These two dynamics seem to carry trans-state relations forward through two trends: on the one hand towards greater contacts across state borders and on the other towards greater particularism around ethnic or national identities.

Despite changing dynamics, trans-state ties are not new to the region. While it is true by definition that trans-state relations "could not occur in an empire" (Krasner, 1995, p. 257), it is worth placing the current debates in the context of the historical reality that "trans-nationalism (as long-distance networks) certainly preceded 'the nation'" (Vertovec, 1999, p. 447). It is meaningful to discuss these as an important force in the region, not because of the novelty of many of its elements but because "transnationalism describes a condition in which, despite great distances and notwithstanding the presence of inter-national borders (and all the laws, regulations and national narratives they represent), certain kind of relationships have been globally intensified and now take place paradoxi-cally in a planet-spanning yet common—however virtual—arena of activity" (Vertovec, 1999, p. 447). We are witnessing a quantitative and qualitative shift in the nature of such activity in the sense that "the dispersed diasporas of old have become today's 'trans-national communities' sustained by a range of modes of social organization, mobility and communication" (Vertovec, 1999, p. 449). Nevertheless, it is worth bearing in mind that as 'precursors' to trans-state actors as defined today (Portes *et al.*, 1999), diasporas have for centuries "been making extensive use of 'old', then 'more modern,' and now 'new' distance-shrinking communications technologies" to sustain trans-state networks (Sheffer, 2003, p. 180).

First, physical and virtual trans-state interaction between individuals, groups and organ-izations in Turkey and the rest of the Balkans has been altered by changes in the means and conditions of communication and movement, framed by the opening up of the region with the demise of the Eastern Bloc. It is now quicker to post your opinion from Istanbul on an internet discussion group tying together members of a regional group across Turkey, the Balkans and Western Europe, which includes activists, association leaders, politicians and academics, than it is to travel to the association's headquarters in the same city. Immigrant associations, to varying degrees, are active on a regional level, involving frequent visits, participation in international events, and the hosting/exchange of various student groups, academic and historic seminars, meetings, theatre and exhibitions across borders. Closer examination of their partners in such activities reveals a bewildering array of contacts, including other branches of their associations, parallel community/civic organizations, religious networks and leaders, military actors, local government officials and institutions, international and national humanitarian organizations, parties and political figures, universities and other educational establishments.

Organizations in Turkey based around religious networks and brotherhoods have also developed their contacts and involvement with various actors in the Balkans in the edu-cational, humanitarian and religious fields. Most prominent is the Gülen movement which, through education and media, has developed a strong presence in the region. The political Islamist movement in Turkey surrounding the National Vision Movement, the Welfare Party, the Virtue Party and most recently the Justice & Development Party have developed contacts with local and national political actors in the region, and colla-borated with other organizations on humanitarian and political questions, often linking religion and questions of identity and persecution in the region, in part to appeal to immi-grant and kin groups. Organizations surrounding the far right, ultra-nationalist movement in Turkey have also been interested in perceived kin, and organizations, publications and think-tanks associated with this movement have made contact with immigrants and kin who fit into their wider visions of a pan-Turkic world stretching 'from the Adriatic to the Wall of China'.

Second, the crises and conflicts surrounding the break-up of Yugoslavia, and the emergence of new states and 'new' minorities and majorities within these states, have also contributed to an increase in trans-state activity. These crises provided points around which much of the activity outlined above could be organized, justified and energised. Most immediately, the conflicts opened up the possibility of humanitarian involvement from Turkey in a variety of forms. This included state and Red Crescent-coordinated campaigns, as well as various initiatives from immigrant associations who collected aid from across Turkey and at times even delivered it to conflict zones themselves. These state and non-state actors also collaborated in the delivery of aid during the wars in Bosnia and Kosovo. The political Islamist movement was also active in this respect. The so-called 'Mercümek scandal' constitutes an infamous example.[11] The Istanbul-based IHH Humanitarian Relief Foundation is also alleged to have ties with the political Islamist movement in Turkey, and has operated in several war zones, including Chechnya and Iraq. The foundation was initially set up in response to the conflict in Bosnia-Herzegovina and has been active in Kosovo.

The conflicts also marked a turning point for many immigrants in Turkey in terms of identification and mobilization, and in some cases towards what could be conceived as a more diasporic identity. The changes in the region in the late 1980s and early 1990s gave a new impetus to immigrant associations (Toumarkaine, 2000). New states and local wars "acted as a factor of communal mobilization ... Up to that date newcomers had been the prime movers in generating intra-communal solidarity but this time it was the long established immigrants who [were] at the forefront of the mobilization" (Toumarkaine, 2000, p. 406). The dynamics of 'widening' and 'narrowing', greater trans-state links and activity, on the one hand, and increased identification with more specific identities, on the other, are inextricably intertwined as acted out by the groups under study. If the conflict in Bosnia-Herzegovina led to a mobilization among those of Bosnian origin in Turkey resulting in greater organization and participation in trans-state networks, it also led them to more narrowly define the parameters of their identification and membership. As a board member of the Bosnia Sandžak Culture & Solidarity Association (BSKDD) remarked in an interview with the author, they had already changed the name of the association from *Yugoslavya* to *Bosna-Sancak* before the idea of Yugoslavia had formally been declared defunct.

In a different way the mobilization of the Kosovar Albanians in Turkey in relation to the situation in Kosovo in the 1990s also constitutes an example of twin pressures and logics bearing on organization and identity. The detoriating situation in Kosovo was key to the mobilization of Albanians in Turkey and served as a key issue around which the community in Turkey could be rallied and rejuvenated (de Rapper, 2001). Yet, at the same time, in order to gain wider support in Turkey, activists were careful to emphasize common interests between Turks and Albanians in Kosovo. A pamphlet distributed by the Turkish–Albanian Brotherhood Culture and Solidarity Association in 1995 asserted that the situation of Albanians and Turks in Kosovo should not be taken separately (TAKKDD, 1995). This stance seems to have been reflected in the association's subsequent efforts to collaborate with other associations and actors, and to cast the Kosovar Albanian nationalist cause in a light compatible with the interests of Turkey and the Turkish minority in Kosovo.

Similar dynamics can be seen in religiously motivated mobilisation. On the one hand, trans-state ties have involved a widening of the dialogue and activities to include a greater number of countries, but on the other these ties have often been along ethno-religious lines, cutting across new states. Political Islamists' ties with Islamists in other Balkan states constitute an example of this cross-border particularism. Yet Islam-related networks do not necessarily limit their activities to Muslims; the Gülen movement has combined religiously inspired trans-state activity with an emphasis on cross-civilizational dialogue and seeking contact with non-Muslim leadership and populations (Yavuz & Esposito, 2003).

The State and Trans-state Ties

Having presented an overview of the actors and processes in play, the second half of the paper deals with a series of questions arising from states' attitudes towards, and involvement in, trans-state ties. The state is inextricably tied into trans-state relations. While it is increasingly hard for practical and normative reasons for the Turkish state to act in foreign policy without taking into account trans-state relations, it is also difficult to disentangle the state from trans-state relations. This is in keeping with recent literature on migration which has pointed to "the very degree to which state institutions co-opt or are at least involved in channelling migrants' transnational practices" and has questioned "whether migrants' transnational practices challenge state institutions or serve their interests" (Ostergaard-Nielsen, 2003, p. 31).

This entanglement manifests itself in many ways; the article addresses three. First, 'human ties' are used in state discourse and policy, and as such are captured by state actors as a tool in foreign policy. Second, historical factors and political culture combine to produce a pervasive statism and nationalism among many non-state actors. Third, state actors can be seen to have 'infiltrated' trans-state relations both in terms of norms and forms. Thus, rather than simply envisaging two separate spheres or processes—inter-state and trans-state—as interacting and shaping each other, we must recognize that to varying degrees they infiltrate each other. The normative and organizational arrangements which form the state (Risse Kappen, 1995) not only shape, but are integral to, trans-state actors and relations.

It is worth placing the following discussion in some theoretical and historical context. In terms of theory a clarification of the relationship between inter-state and trans-state ties is necessary. First, greater trans-state ties do not entail the demise or weakening of the state *per se*. I concur with critics who challenge "the implication that the nation-state has diminished in significance as a unit of social analysis" (Jackson *et al.*, 2004, p. 4) as "one can subscribe to the proposition that national governments are extremely significant in international relations and still claim that transnational actors crucially affect state interests, policies, and inter-state relations" (Risse-Kappen, 1995, pp. 14–15).

Second, this assumption seems related to a wider neglect of the state as a concept, as a polity and as an actor. Until recently IR studies of transnational relations have "mostly neglect[ed] structures of governance, in particular the state" (Risse-Kappen, 1995, p. 16). Likewise, in anthropology, "implicit in athropological studies of transnational processes is the work of the 'state', as for example the guardian of national borders, the arbiter of citizenship, and the entity responsible for foreign policy" (Kearney, 1999, p. 521), yet here too state actors and institutions have often been ignored.

Third, any theoretical discussion of trans-state relations must clarify its conceptualization of the state. The state here is understood as comprising a set of actors and institutions which are perceived to constitute the state, and as a major constituent of the legal, geographical, ideological and ideational context within which state and non-state actors exist. It follows from this definition that the state should not simply be considered as an actor (or rather set of actors) but as a key element of the environment in which various actors operate. Furthermore, if we return to Keohane and Nye's definition of 'transnational relations', the reference of exclusion is in fact not to the 'state' but to the 'central foreign policy organs of government'. It is not therefore paradoxical to locate the state in trans-state relations, given that the sprawling Turkish state consists of a variety of actors and structures outside these central organs which are also involved in external relations.

That the state as a normative and institutional force is prevalent, at times dominant, in trans-state relations is more comphrensible in the light of historical developments. The gradual contraction and collapse of the Ottoman Empire and a series of wars shaped immigration. Yet more generally states have been key actors in the movement of peoples—be it forced or encouraged movement, settlement and exile around, and in and out of, the Balkans. Ottoman state practices can be seen to have been superseded by national states which were no less eager to move populations to fit their nation-building projects and policies. The official forced population exchange between Greece and Turkey followed by bilateral agreements signed between Turkey and Balkan states regarding voluntary immigration constitute clear examples. On the flipside the subsequent policy of balancing Istanbul's Greeks/Orthodox Christians with Western Thrace's Turks/Muslims (exempt from the exchange) involved discouraging inward immigration in keeping with perceived state policy and interests.

Hugh Poulton characterizes the more recent Turkish government line as being that, while Turkey remains a potential home in times of extreme hardship, it would be better if outside groups remain citizens of their respective states and act as a link to Turkey (1997a). This can be seen as parallel to the way in which views in Turkey of the significant number of Turkish citizens living in Western Europe have changed, as state priorities have, "from 'remittance machines' to 'Euro Turks'" (Ostergaard-Nielsen, 2003, p. 107). Furthermore, internally Turkish policy makers have viewed the question of settlement of immigrants partly through the lens of their overall aim of consolidating Anatolia as a Muslim Turkish homeland (Kirisci, 1995; Yildiz, 2001). In sum, for centuries the question of immigration and population movement has been tied up closely with state power and interests, and with imperial and national visions of security and stability. Long before human security became a vogue topic in IR imperial and national elites eyed immigrants and 'kin' in the Balkans as components of their strategies for security, stability and leverage in politics. It is against this historical background, in which states play such a central role, that the developments below can be better understood.

The 'Human Ties' Theme in State Policy

İnsani bağlar (human ties) have been captured by the state as a discursive tool in foreign policy. These, together with cultural and historical ties, have been repeatedly referred to by state actors to explain state stances on developments in the Balkans in the 1990s and the first half of the 2000s. State representatives explain Turkish Balkan policy both internally and externally by referring to kin in the region and immigrants in Turkey. To cite just a few examples, the importance Turkey attaches to the region, Turkey's approach to the Stability Pact, Turkey's concern over the situation in Kosovo, as with Bosnia and Herzegovina previously, Turkey's decision to offer refugee status to Kosovar refugees, Turkey's inclusion in the UN Secretary General's Kosovo Friendship Group, its relations with Bulgaria, Macedonia and so on are all in official discourse linked to Turkey's 'human ties' with the region, or with the 'bridges of friendship' that such populations constitute. Sometimes human ties are listed as one of several factors, sometimes they are cited as the first among many, and in some instances they have been the sole explanation Turkish officials have given for Turkish involvement or policy.

While such references can partly be seen as a response to the pressures upon state actors from 'kin' and 'immigrants', as well as more general public pressure, state actors' tendency to ignore such pressure where it contradicts perceived state interests suggests that repeated references are also used to justify rather than simply explain regional policy. Turkey's concerns at being side-lined from the European security architecture emerging in the 1990s, bilateral competition and tension with Greece, and Turkey's partnership with the USA seem to have all been key to how Turkey has viewed, responded to and acted in relation to developments in the Balkans. Furthermore, fears over the influence of other states from the Middle East have been behind to Turkey's attempts at outreach to Muslim communities throughout the region. In particular, fears that Islamic Wahhabism, promoted by Saudi Arabia and closely tied up with the inflow of foreign aid and capital into the region, might dislodge a more liberal Balkan Islam, perceived in Turkey as an Ottoman legacy, has spurred Turkish state (and non-state) activities.[12]

Yet, at the level of discourse, policy makers have preferred to emphasize historical, cultural and human links rather than make explicit the ties between Turkish involvement and engagement and its long-term multilateral and bilateral objectives. In this sense these human ties can be seen to have provided a convenient set of themes on which policy makers could draw when it suited them, but which they could ignore or treat evasively when they did not desire to, or could not meet the demands of the kin and immigrants seemingly so important to Turkey's position. In this sense 'human ties' as a concept and political buzzword was captured by the state. That at times the stance of state actors is accepted at face value by non-state actors themselves, even endorsed, can only be explained in full if we look at the wider ideological context in which both state and non-state actors are operating. In the next section I will look in particular at statism and nationalism as key to this context.

Statism and Trans-state Actors

Statism and nationalism are pervasive in the political culture of Turkey and the wider region.[13] This section aims to draw attention to the striking degree to which some non-state actors employ, and even it seems embrace, statism and official nationalism in their activities. RTKDD, established in 1950 in Istanbul as Vardarlılar Yardımlaşma Derneği (People from Vardar Mutual Assistance Association), changing its name in 1967, is one of the few associations not closed during the military coup periods. It is one of 334 founding members of the Rumeli Turks Culture & Solidarity Foundation (RUTEV) set up in 1996. The RTKDD has prided itself as constituting a bridge between Macedonia and Turkey, and RUTEV on such a role region-wide. Both organizations are increasingly involved in trans-state activities between Turkey and Macedonia, with substantial links to the political and social institutions of the Turks of Macedonia. Yet states and state power seem key in the world-view of these organisations—be it the Ottoman state to which they make numerous references, or the states of the region today with which they are keen to maintain contacts. They are particularly proud of recognition from both states and have been eager to participate in bilateral relations. In March 2002 the RTKDD hosted the Istanbul leg of an official visit to Turkey of the late Macedonian president Boris Trajkovski, and in May 2001 it hosted an official visit by the Inter-parliamentary Macedonian Friendship Group.

This concern seems to reflect a wider ideological disposition towards states as the key actors in the politics of the region. The most striking aspect of both organizations is their aparent immersion in official Turkish nationalism and statism. The symbols and discourse are remarkably similar to those of a state institution—in particular with respect to the Turkish flag and founder of the republic Mustafa Kemal Ataturk. While the RTKDD may constitute an extreme form of such nationalist statist trans-state activity (Toumarkaine, 2000), it has been quite successful in steering a variety of connected associations in the same direction through collaborative activities. For example, the association led the organization of a series of events to celebrate the 650th anniversary of entry into the Balkans.[14] While focused on the Turkish presence in the Balkans, statist symbols were overtly referred to throughout the proceedings.[15] The logic of this combination is communicated in the protocol: "We, the associations representing Rumeli people see ourselves as the natural heirs of Mustafa Kemal Ataturk, founder of the Turkish Republic".

As suggested by the wider collaboration surrounding the event, it can be placed within varying degrees of statism among immigrant and Balkan organizations, even in those in which it might not be so readily expected, such as the 'People from Pristina Culture & Solidarity Association' and BSKDD. While these organizations steer clear of the overt Turkism of the RTKDD, given the respective Albanian and Bosnian ethnic origins of most members, clear examples of statism can be found in the trans-state and domestic activities and discourse of the associations. The recent reaction of the latter in relation to state broadcasting in the Bosnian language in June 2004 offers interesting clues into how the association envisages its place in relation to the Turkish state and nationalism. After the launch of a new programme slot on state television channel TRT3 in response to pressures for broadcasting in minority languages, many Bosnian associations responding to the Bosnian version of the slot expressed surprise and criticism. In an advertisement sent to the major newspapers, 12 associations and foundations stated:

FROM THE BOSNIA-SANDZAK FOUNDATIONS AND ASSOCIATIONS TO THE GREAT TURKISH NATION. We see that when TRT was making a decision to broadcast in different languages, Bosnian was included among these languages. This decision and practice was a surprise for us ... We are a community that have mixed like 'SKIN AND NAIL' for centuries with all the people of the Turkish Republic, the greatest legacy left to us by the Great Leader ATATURK. We support with all our heart the spirit and understanding of ATATURK'S expression "HOW HAPPY IS HE WHO CALLS HIMSELF A TURK" and carry our TURKISH identity with pride. (Bosnia Sandžak Foundations and Associations, 2004)

They go on to state, while thanking the state for this cultural service, that they do not want to be part of a perceived attempt to divide Turkey along ethnic lines or be perceived as a 'minority', both references to Kurdish political and cultural claims, and international pressure on the issue. They suggest that the programme be aired on TRT International, a trans-state channel to further links with those 'brothers' left in Bosnia and Sandžak (Bosnia Sandžak Foundations and Associations, 2004).[16] This episode is just one of the more obvious that reveals the degree of statism and nationalism among various Balkan-related groups in Turkey.

Similar dynamics seem to be applicable to the religiously inspired Gülen movement active in the Balkans. As Berna Turam has pointed out in her study of the Kazak–Turk Education Foundation active in Kazakhstan, there is no contradiction in the foundation being a civil society agent that defines itself as a servant of the state (Turam, 2003, p. 194). As she argues, while its "capacity to organize itself without being organized by the state" (Calhoun, cited in Turam, 2003, p. 194) means it fits one definition of civil society, a close identification of the nation with the state and "primary identification with the nation" by its followers results in the community expanding "its sphere of influence and power outside national borders *because* of its national loyalties, not despite them" (Turam, 2003, pp. 194–195). Thus, across a variety of non-state actors, statism finds its way into trans-state relations. As an idealized concept that is reproduced, the state shapes perceptions, understandings and action.

Yet while statism and nationalism offer two explanations for the propensity of non-state actors to refer to and collaborate with state actors, it is worth emphasizing that, beyond ideological factors, more practical issues are also relevant. One factor is the lack of alternative partners. In a May 2004 interview published in *Yeni Dönem*, a Turkish newspaper in Kosovo, Liriye Gas, the head of *Hanımeli*, a Kosovo Turkish Women's Association, complained that all potential donors they approached for funding for projects pointed them in the direction of the Turkish state and other Turkish organizations in Kosovo:

> I was generally met with the following words, "Your project is really quite good but let us leave it for a later period". They also showed us an address . . . We were met by the foreign donors with [the words], "But you are not alone. You have the Turks, the Turkish state, institutions that have come from Turkey behind you, you can ask for help from them."[17]

Thus, for pragmatic reasons, it seems that many non-state actors have chosen to embrace the state as a partner.

Yet another factor is the pressure upon civil society actors to avoid breaking taboos enshrined in the Turkish constitution and the law regarding particular identities or organization around them. Overall, it is impossible to specify confidently in any given case whether statism is a means or an end in the discourse and activities of non-state actors. As Yasin Aktay has noted in relation to the Islamic Gülen movement, "it is very difficult to distinguish sincere nationalism from a clientele relation with the state" (2003, p. 149). This is related to a wider phenomenon, as Krasner states: "the character of transnational actors will reflect the institutional environment within which they must function and the most important component of this environment is states" (Krasner, 1995, p. 258). As envisaged theoretically by Krasner, non-state actors in Turkey conform in key ways to the institutional framework and norms of the Turkish state in order to operate (1995). The statism of non-state actors can also be seen in this light, as can their nationalism and conservative stance on a variety of questions. Furthermore, institutionally they seek to conform to acceptable formats and activities, and their workings are shaped by the rules and regulations governing associations and foundations currently undergoing significant change. This is most notably in the form of article 5 of the association law, last amended in January 2003, which outlaws the foundation of associations that aim to create in the republic racial, religious, sectarian or regional difference or minorities based on such differences, or to damage the unitary state structure of the republic. The task of analysing all these dynamics is complicated further by the stance of the Turkish state, and its use of non-state actors and the discourse and modus operandi of trans-state ties in its own policy, to which I now turn.

The State in a Trans-state Mould

In this section I will tentatively explore whether it is useful to conceive of the Turkish state as having adopted some of the norms and forms we associate with trans-state activity as part of its policy towards the Balkans. In addition to the pressures on non-state actors to conform to the conditions of the polity, it is also possible to talk of state isomorphism, an effort on the part of certain actors and institutions within the state to conform to the forms and norms of trans-state activity in an effort to work with, or even from within, this sphere. This is part of a wider phenomenon in Turkey in which the state has sought to legitimize itself and its ideology through the guise of civil society. As Navaro-Yashin has demonstrated, in the 1990s the state "demanded a realm of civil society in favor of itself" (2002, p. 119) while "a discourse of civil society became instrumental in claims for legitimate ownership of state power" (2002, p. 136). She argues that the discourses of civil society and state are "enmeshed, intermerged, rendered inherent to one another" on the ground to such a degree that the analytical distinction is rendered obsolete (1998, p. 21; 2002). For our purposes it seems useful to identify the twin processes of state isomorphism and non-state isomorphism as together constituting 'mutual isomorphism'. Here I wish to dwell on three examples of what might be considered examples of state isomorphism. First, the work of the Turkish State Religious Directorate and Religious Foundation is examined. Second, the implications of overlap in state and non-state interests in the sphere of education are taken up. Third, the activities of the Turkish Cooperation and Development Agency (TIKA) and of the Turkish armed forces deployed in the region are discussed.

The work of DİB, which operates as a sub-unit of the Prime Ministry but which wields a substantial budget dwarfing many other ministries, deserves attention.[18] It has facilitated a series of links with Muslim communities in the region. These include multilateral initiatives such as the Eurasian Islamic assemblies organized by the directorate, the first three of which were held in Turkey in 1995, 1996 and 1998, bringing together religious representatives from across Eastern Europe, the Caucasus and Central Asia, as well as bilateral links through visits and cooperation between religious leaders, and appointment of religious services counsellors to various consulates abroad.[19] Details of visits by religious leaders and other representatives are outlined in the monthly *Diyanet*, revealing a variety of contacts with religious actors in the region. It also directs various 'services', spanning religious services, education and scholarships, humanitarian aid, support for the restoration and building of mosques, and publications in a range of languages, towards the *dindaş* and *soydaş*, those of common religion and ethnicity respectively, including those in the Balkans.

Confusingly, although quite relevant to this discussion, the Religious Foundation, established in 1975, despite its name and status as a pious foundation, is closely connected to, and financially intertwined with, the directorate. The Head of DİB is also the head of the foundation board of trustees, and the foundation is a key source of funds for the directorate. As a recent report underlines, the relationship between the two has undergone significant changes in recent years, although both institutions remain largely non-transparent and unaccountable in their national and international activities (Cakir & Bozan, 2005). The foundation has also been active in the Balkans. In 1994 the board travelled throughout the region on an exploratory trip, visiting communities, meeting local religious leadership in cities and towns and visiting religious monuments and institutions.[20] The foundation has worked closely with official partners, including the religious affairs directorate, the foreign ministry and Turkish Red Crescent in administering aid in the Balkans. It has also provided the resources for education projects in the Balkans, including a religious institute in Sofia and schools in Romania and Bulgaria, and provided scholarships in the field for study in Turkey, working again closely with ministries and the Council for Higher Education.

Second, to dwell on this last example, in the area of education clear overlap, competition and collaboration between state institutions and non-state actors can be seen. There has been much speculation over the educational activities of the "faith inspired education movement" led, and inspired, by Fethullah Gülen (Yavuz, 2003b, p. 19) which has set up a series of schools and institutes throughout the region. The relationship between this network and the Turkish state is a complex one. While the end of the 1990s saw the movement come under increasing scrutiny and suspicion from state officials, in particular the military, and Fethullah Gülen was officially investigated in Turkey, the network can also claim support from within some political circles in Turkey and notably preaches a blend of Islamic identity and Turkish nationalism which is not radically different at first glance from the Turk-Islamic synthesis of the Turkish state of the 1980s and early 1990s. An increase in the number of students pursuing higher education in Turkey is an area where the interests of immigrant groups, religious groups and state actors have overlapped. Balkan immigrant networks have been active in providing scholarships and support for students from the region. To give an idea of the scale of change, 1994–98 saw an increase in students from Bosnia-Herzegovina from 92 to 601 (down to 414 in 2000) and from Macedonia from 88 in 1994 to 421 by the end of the decade. The increase was even greater in the case of Albania: from 55 in 1994 to 992 in 1998 (down to 779 in 2000). These numbers are striking given that in the late 1990s more than half the citizens of Bosnia-Herzegovina, Macedonia and Albania officially residing in Turkey were students (State Institute of Statistics, 2002). While it serves state interests to be seen a cultural or educational leader in the region, more general concerns about keeping a tight grip on education, for example fears about the Gülen network's impact within Turkey on higher education and society, complicate the picture significantly.

Third, even from within the 'central foreign policy organs of government' signs of attempts to downplay the image of the state and establish powerful trans-state ties is evident. TİKA can be seen as an active state agency which has taken on the outside attributes of a non-state actor. Even its name suggests efforts to move beyond the image of a cumbersome state institution. It promotes itself and is primarily known as TİKA, despite the administrative name of the entity, the Economic, Cultural, Education and Technical Cooperation Directorate, administered within the budget of the Ministry of Foreign Affairs. With coordinator offices in Albania, Bosnia-Herzegovina and Kosovo the agency constitutes an important actor and focus for state initiatives in relation to these countries. The Turkish armed forces, through their presence in the region as part of peace-keeping missions and as a bilateral partner in various agreements and protocols encouraging cross-border contact, has demonstrated that even a military state actor can operate with, and in a seemingly similar format to, non-state actors, making contact with local populations in a hearts-and-minds-style policy.[21] Overall, various state actors have to varying degrees adopted the forms and methods of trans-state actors in their efforts to establish and maintain ties with the region.

Conclusion

In conclusion, trans-state relations between Turkey and the rest of the Balkans since 1989 have been characterized by substantial qualitative and quantitative changes. At the same time the state has remained in many respects a key force in, and through these dynamics. The above account has attempted to weave together theoretical insights with the particularities of the case at hand. It seems worthwhile to attempt to situate these findings within broader concerns regarding transnationalization and Europeanization in the region. The developments outlined in the first half of the paper should be read in conjunction with the 'reservations' outlined in the second half. In this sense, in the same way that we must reject the fallacy of Europeanization as the demise of the state as a crucial actor in Western European politics (Milward, 1992; Moravcsik, 1999), we must be wary of assuming that the intensification of trans-state relations coupled with Europeanization signals the demise of the Balkan state. We still face state actors and statism as significant forces in shaping the terms of an evolving Europe. Yet, as I have outlined above, this does not make trans-state relations any less relevant or significant. As Risse-Kappen puts it, "one does not have to do away with the 'state' to establish the influence of transnational relations in world politics" (1995, p. 15). Previous oversight seems partly related to the fact that, as academics searching for an alternative to the destructive statism and nationalism in the region, we may read certain overall logics into trans-state dynamics where no single logic exists. We cannot assume that, because actors operate across a region, they support regional integration, or a particular EU-centred vision of regional integration and stability. Various actors have quite specific visions of what constitutes desirable regional stability and integration, and are wary of and cynical about, sometimes openly hostile towards, alternative visions. Most fundamentally, the trans-state relations examined in this paper do not carry the region in any single direction. The multiplicity of actors and networks highlight a wide array of ideas and aims, memories and identities competing for voice and space in this dynamic region.

Acknowledgements

This article is based on a paper presented at the 'Transnationalism in the Balkans' Conference organized by LSE and the Ost-Europa Institute Berlin in London in November 2004. I am grateful to the organizers and participants, and to my superviser Prof. Anthony Smith, for their feedback. I would also like to thank the Ernest Gellner Memorial Fund, which made part of the fieldwork possible.

Notes

1. 'Nation-state' is a problematic term given its implications of congruity of state and nation. For the rest of the article the less value-laden term 'state' will be used.

2. Furthermore, it has been argued that "transnational and global phenomena conflict with the jurisdiction and power of states and are what might be called 'trans-statal'"; nevertheless "this term has not gained common usage" (Kearney, 1999, p. 521).

3. However, as will become clear in the article, other groups and forms of identification, also of complex constitution and delineation, such as Islamists, nationalists, Turkist-'Idealists' are also significant actors in trans-state ties. I rely in approaching these ideologies and identities on the invaluable work of various scholars of Turkish identity, in particular Bora (1995, 1997, 1998) (for an English summary see Bora (2003)), Kadioglu (1996) on official nationalism, Yavuz (2003a) and Gole (1996) on Islamist and Islamic movements.

4. In the Balkans the Christian Gagauz Turks constitute an example of an exception of the assumed inclusion of all Turks in a wider set of Muslim populations. For Turkey's policy on links with, and the immigration to Turkey of, Gagauz Turks, see Kirisci (1995). More widely, the question of non-Muslim (and non-Sunni Muslim) Turkish citizens and Turks is a crucial component of wider questions of identity and citizenship in Turkey.

5. See Kumbetoglu (1997) for findings from Bosnian refugees. I am grateful to Prof. Sule Kut for drawing my attention to the variety of political implications resulting from such perceived or actual liability. See Kut (2000).

6. *Göç-Der* (1999) citing Filiz Doğanay of the State Statistical Institute.

7. Having said this, the term 'Balkan göçmeni' is used to specify Balkan origins and is used frequently.

8. I am grateful to Vangelis Kechriotis for drawing my attention to this alternative example.

9. On these 'national histories', see the edited volume published by the Center for Democracy and Reconciliation in Southeast Europe (Koulouri, 2002). The Center itself constitutes an example of a successful trans-state region-wide initiative.

10. In the foreword to the published proceedings of the May–June 2002 650 Yil Symposium (Aganoglu, 2002).

11. Scandal over the mispropriation of aid collected by the Welfare Party and National Vision movement for Bosnian Muslims during the war.

12. This influence has appeared through extreme religious networks centred arround mosques or individuals connected with the Wahhabi movement in Bosnia-Herzegovina, Sandžak, Kosovo, Albania and Macedonia, as well as through foreign Islamist volunteers in the region's conflicts.

13. It is worth emphasizing the intertwining of nationalism and statism, making it problematic to surgically dissect them. Yashin-Navaro defines "statism as something beyond nationalism, as an identification not only or even necessarily with a nation, but with a reified and exalted state" (2002, p. 201). It might in fact be better to see the two as locked into a mutually reinforcing symbiotic relationship.

14. Thirty-three associations, two foundations and the Rumeli Federation were listed as the organizing institutions, yet the preparation commission reveals a more limited set of actors centred around officers of the RTKDD.

15. The symposium also received financial and organizational support from the Turkish state.

16. The Turkish media took up the issue in detail with a variety of takes on its implications. See, for example, *Radikal*, 8 June 2004; *Milliyet*, 7 June 2004; *Sabah*, 5 June 2004; and *Hürriyet*, 17 June 2004.

17. Cited in Gucluturk (2004; author's translation from Turkish).

18. On the political significance of the Directorate see Cizre-Sakallioglu (1996).

19. For details, see the proceedings in DİB (1996, 1998, 2000). The Fourth assembly was held in July 2000 in Sarajevo, the fifth in 2002 in Magosa, Northern Cyprus and the sixth in 2005 in Istanbul.

20. A book describing the trip, *Tuna Nehri Konuşsaydı* (If the Danube spoke), written by Halit Güler (deputy head of the foundation), was published by the Foundation Publishers in 1995. It won the 1996 Turkish Writers Union Award for Travel writing, and is currently in its second edition.

21. On the role of the Turkish military in foreign policy and politics see Insel & Bayramoglu (2004), especially the contribution by Ilhan Uzgel (2004). For an overview of actors in Turkish foreign policy, including the military, see Robins (2003).

References

Aganoglu, Y. (Ed.) (2002) *650. Yıl Sempozyumu: Türklerin Rumeli'ye Çıkışının 650. Yıldönümü* (650th Year Symposium: 650th Anniversary of Turks' Entry into Rumeli) (Istanbul: RTKDD).

Aktay, Y. (2003) Diaspora and stability: constitutive elements in a body of knowledge, in: M. H. Yavuz & J. L. Esposito (Eds), *Turkish Islam and the Secular State: The Gulen Movement*, pp. 131–155 (Syracuse, NY: Syracuse University Press).

Bora, T. (1995) Turkish national identity, Turkish nationalism and the Balkan problem, in: G. G. Ozdogan & K. Saybasili (Eds), *Balkans: A Mirror of the New International Order* (Eren: Istanbul).

Bora, T. (1997) *Milliyetçiliğin Kara Baharı* (The Black Spring of Nationalism) (Istanbul: Birikim Yayınları).

Bora, T. (1998) *Türk sağının Üç Hali: Milliyetçilik, Muhafazakarlık, İslamcılık* (The Three States of the Turkish Right: Nationalism, Conservatism, Islamism) (Istanbul: Birikim Yayınları).

Bora, T. (2003) Nationalist discourses in Turkey, *South Atlantic Quarterly*, 102(2–3), pp. 433–451.

Bosnia-Sandžak Foundations & Associations (2004) *Bosna Sancak Vakıf ve Derneklerinden Yüce Türk Milletine* (From the Bosnia-Sandžak Foundations and Associations to the Great Turkish Nation), advertisement in *Hürriyet*, 17 June 2004.

Brubaker, R. (1996) *Nationalism Reframed: Nationhood and the National Question in the New Europe* (Cambridge: Cambridge University Press).

Cakir, R. & Bozan, I. (2005) *Sivil Şeffaf ve Demokratik Bir Diyanet İşleri Başkanlığı Mümkün Mü'* (Is a Civil, Transparent and Democratic Religious Directorate Possible?), TESEV Report (Istanbul: TESEV Yayınları).

Cizre Sakallıoğlu, Ü. (1996) Parameters and strategies of Islam–state interaction in Republican Turkey, *International Journal of Middle East Studies*, 28, pp. 231–251.

De Rapper, G. (2001) *Les Albanais à Istanbul*, Dossiers de l'IFEA no. 3 (Istanbul: IFEA).

Diyanet İşleri Başkanlığı (DİB—Religious Affairs Directorate) (1996) *I. Avrasya İslam Şurası*, 23–25 October 1995, Ankara (Ankara: T. C. Diyanet İşleri Başkanlığı).

DİB (1998) *II. Avrasya İslam Şurası*, 21–24 October 1996, Istanbul (Ankara: T. C. Diyanet İşleri Başkanlığı).

DİB (2000) *III. Avrasya İslam Şurası*, 25–29 May 1998, Ankara (Ankara: T. C. Diyanet İşleri Başkanlığı).

Göç-Der (1999) *Göç-Der Haber Bülteni*, 2(13), magazine published by Göç-Der: Göç Edenler Sosyal Yardımlaşma ve Kültür Derneği.

Gole, N. (1996) *Forbidden Modern: Civilization and Veiling* (Ann Arbor, MI: University of Michigan Press).

Gucluturk, T. (2004) Yabancı bağışçılar tarafından Kosova Türk Kadın Derneklerine Ayrımcılık Yapılıyor (Kosovo Turkish women's associations are being discriminated against by foreign donors), *Kosova Yeni Dönem Gazetesi*, 6 May 2004.

Guler, H. (1995) *Tuna Nehri Konuşsaydı* (If the Danube Could Talk) (Ankara: Türkiye Diyanet Vakfı Yayınları).

Insel, A. & Bayramoglu, A. (Eds) (2004) *Türkiye'de Ordu* (The Military in Turkey) (Istanbul: Birikim Yayınları).

Jackson, P., Crang, P. & Dwyer, C. (2004) Introduction: the spaces of transnationality, in: P. Jackson *et al.* (Eds), *Transnational Spaces* (London: Routledge).

Kadioglu, A. (1996) The paradox of Turkish nationalism and the construction of official identity, *Middle East Studies*, 32, pp. 177–193.

Karpat, K. (2002) *The Politicization of Islam: Reconstructing Identity, State, Faith, and Community in the late Ottoman State* (New York: Oxford University Press).

Kearney, M. (1999) The local and the global: the anthropology of globalization and transnationalism, reprinted in: S. Vertovec & R. Cohen (Eds), *Migration, Diasporas and Transnationalism* (Cheltenham: Edward Elgar Publishing).

Keohane, R. & Nye, J. (1971) Introduction, in: Keohane & Nye (Eds), *Transnational Relations and World Politics* (Cambridge, MA: Harvard University Press).

Kirisci, K. (1995) Post Second World War immigration from Balkan countries to Turkey, *New Perspectives on Turkey*, 12, pp. 61–77.

Koulouri, C. (Ed.) (2002) *Clio in the Balkans: The Politics of History Education* (Thessaloniki: Center for Democracy and Reconciliation in Southeast Europe).

Krasner, S. D. (1995) Power politics, institutions and transnational relations, in: T. Risse-Kappen (Ed.), *Bringing Transnational Relations back in: Non-state Actors, Domestic Structures and International Institutions* (Cambridge: Cambridge University Press).

Kumbetoglu, B. (1997) Göçmen ve Sığınmacı Gruplardan bir Kesit: Bulgaristan Göçmenleri ve Bosnalı Sığınmacılar (A cross-section from a group of immigrants and refugees: immigrants from Bulgaria and Bosnian refugees), in: K. Saybaşılı & G. Özcan (Eds), *Yeni Balkanlar, Eski Sorunlar* (New Balkans, Old Problems) (Istanbul: Bağlam Yayınları).

Kut, Ş. (2000) Turks of Kosovo: what to expect?, *Perceptions: Journal of International Affairs*, 5(3).

Milward, A. (1992) *The European Rescue of the Nation-State* (London: Routledge).

Moravcsik, A. (1999) *The Choice for Europe: Social Purpose and State Power from Messina to Maastricht* (London: University College London Press).

Navaro-Yashin, Y. (1998) Uses and abuses of 'state and civil society' in contemporary Turkey, *New Perspectives on Turkey*, 18(2), pp. 1–22.

Navaro-Yashin, Y. (2002) *Faces of the State: Secularism and Public Life in Turkey* (Princeton, NJ: Princeton University Press).

Nichols, T., Sugur, N. & Sugur, S. (2003) Muhacir Bulgarian workers in Turkey: their relation to management and fellow workers in the formal employment sector, *Middle Eastern Studies*, 39(2), pp. 37–54.

Norris, H. (1993) *Islam in the Balkans: Religion and Society between Europe and the Arab World* (London: Hurst).

Ostergaard-Neilsen, E. (2003) *Transnational Politics: Turks and Kurds in Germany* (London: Routledge).

Oxfeld, E. & Long, L. D. (2004) Introduction: an ethnography of return, in: L. D. Long & E. Oxfeld (Eds), *Coming Home? Refugees, Migrants and Those Who Stayed Behind* (Philadelphia, PA: University of Pennsylvania Press).

Portes, A., Guarnizo, L. E. & Landolt, P. (1999) The study of transnationalism: pitfalls and promise of an emergent research field, *Ethnic & Racial Studies*, 22(2), pp. 447–462.

Poulton, H. (1997a) Turkey as a kin-state: Turkish foreign policy towards Turkish and Muslim communities in the Balkans, in: H. Poulton & S. Taji-Farouki (Eds), *Muslim Identity and the Balkan State* (London: Hurst).

Poulton, H. (1997b) *Top Hat, Grey Wolf and Crescent: Turkish Nationalism and the Turkish Republic* (London: Hurst).

Poulton, H. & Taji-Farouki, S. (Eds) (1997) *Muslim Identity and the Balkan State* (London: Hurst).

Risse-Kappen, T. (1995) Bringing transnational relations back in: introduction, in: Risse-Kappen (Ed.), *Bringing Transnational Relations back in: Non-state Actors, Domestic Structures and International Institutions* (Cambridge: Cambridge University Press).

Robins, P. (2003) *Suits and Uniforms: Turkish Foreign Policy since the Cold War* (Seattle, WA: University of Washington Press).

Sheffer, G. (2003) *Diaspora Politics: At Home Abroad* (Cambridge: Cambridge University Press).

State Instititute of Statistics (2002) *Statistical Yearbook of Turkey 2001* (Ankara: State Instititute of Statistics).

Toumarkaine, A. (2000) Balkan and Caucasian immigrant associations: community and politics, in: S. Yersimos et al. (Eds), *Civil Society in the Grip of Nationalism: Studies of Political Culture in Contemporary Turkey* (Istanbul: Orient Institut/IFEA).

Turam, B. (2003) National loyalties and international undertakings: the case of the Gulen community in Kazakhstan, in: H. Yavuz & J. Esposito (Eds), *Turkish Islam and the Secular State: The Gulen Movement* (Syracuse, NY: Syracuse University Press).

Turk-Arnavut Kardesligi Kultur ve Dayanisma Dernegi (TAKKDD) (1995) *Kosova Sorunu* (The Kosovo Problem) (Istanbul: TAKKDD).

Uzgel, I. (2004) Ordu Dis Politikanin Neresinde? (Where in foreign policy is the army?), in: A. Insel & A. Bayramoglu (Eds), *Türkiye'de Ordu* (The Military in Turkey) (Istanbul: Birikim Yayınları).

Van Hear, N. (1998) *New Diasporas: The Mass Exodus, Dispersal and Regrouping of Migrant Communities* (London: University College London Press).

Vertovec, S. (1999) Conceiving and researching transnationalism, *Ethnic & Racial Studies*, 22(2), pp. 447–462.

Yavuz, H. (2003a) *Islamic Political Identity in Turkey* (Oxford: Oxford University Press).

Yavuz, H. (2003b) The Gulen movement: Turkish puritans, in: M. H. Yavuz & J. L. Esposito (Eds), *Turkish Islam and the Secular State: The Gulen Movement*, pp. 19–47 (Syracuse, NY: Syracuse University Press).

Yavuz, M. H. & Esposito, J. L. (Eds) (2003) *Turkish Islam and the Secular State: The Gulen Movement* (Syracuse, NY: Syracuse University Press).

Yildiz, A. (2001) *'Ne Mutlu Türküm Diyebilene': Turk Ulusal Kimliğinin Etno-Seküler Sınırları (1919–1938)* ('How Happy is He Who Can Call Himself a Turk': The Ethno-Secular Boundaries of Turkish National Identity) (Istanbul: İletişim Yayınları).

Index

Agamben, G. 28, 37
Aktay, Y. 104
Anamorava 49, 50
Anderson, J. 2
Arizona market; Bosnia and Herzegovina
    31–2

Bajaga, M. Bajagić 66, 73
Baker, C. 51
Balašević, D. 64–6
Batt, J. 11
Beck, U. 2
Beljo, A. 84–5
Bete, N. 69
borders; merchants and informal
    transnationalism 27–40
Bosnia and Herzegovina 39, 81; Arizona
    market 31–2; lawlessness 37
Bosnia Sandžak Culture and Solidarity
    Association (BSKDD) 99, 103–4
Bosnia-Herzegovina 8, 53
Bougarel, X. 66
Brčko 31–2
Brena, L. 68, 70, 71, 72
Brubaker, R. 53, 97
Bulgaria 11

Calic, M.-J. 9
Carothers, T. 47, 49
Celebi, E. 29–30
cigarette smuggling 34–5
civil society; Kosovo 41–57
Cocozelli, F. 48
Cohen, A. 69
Council for the Defence of Human
    Rights and Freedoms (CDHRF) 44
Croatia 4, 5, 7, 18, 51; confiscation of memory
    64; diaspora involvement 82–6; musical
    activity in Serbia-Montenegro 61–2;
    musical activity in Slovenia 62–3;
    transnational ties 79–91;
    Yugo-nostalgia 65

Croatian Democratic Union (HDZ) 64,
    84, 85, 87
Croatian diaspora 82–6; Croatian World
    Congress 84, 85; and democratic
    transition 85; Gotovina issue 85; and
    homeland Croatians 86–8; Law on
    Croatian Citizenship 83–4; Ministry of
    Return and Immigration 84; post-2000
    marginalization 84–5
cultural spaces; transnational 59–61

democratization: historical legacy 10–11;
    international aspect 11–12; post-
    communist transition approaches 8–12;
    stateness dimension 11, 12
Dežulović, B. 67
diaspora engagement; transnational
    actors 18–19
Dragićević-Šešić, M. 71
Dragović D. 61
drug trafficking 34
Duffield, M. 19

economic reforms; impact 16–18
ethnic networks; and the weak state 12–13, 21
ethno-multiculturalism; post-socialist
    states 52–5
European Security and Defence Policy
    (ESDP) 9
European Union (EU) 3, 5, 50; criticisms of
    approach 21–2; enlargement 7; full
    membership 21; state-building agenda 9
Europeanization 3, 4, 5, 7–25; common state
    legacy 13–14; enhanced conditionality 9;
    European Security and Defence Policy
    (ESDP) 9; interconnectedness 10; legacy
    of war and its political economy 14–16;
    liberal economic reforms 16–18; post-
    communist transition approaches 8–12;
    stability dilemma 9; Stabilization and
    Association process (SAp) 8–9, 16; state
    weakness and ethnic networks 12–13;